"How sad to see so much confu [barcode]
is proof one is Protestant. Davi
site: our Protestant fathers were zealous believers
God has manifested himself through natural revelation, and natural
law is an indispensable aspect. As the public square spirals, natural
law could not be more relevant. Without it, we lose the ability to
persuade non-Christians of a moral framework so critical to the
survival of human dignity and a just society. Employing natural law
in the public square can be intimidating, but VanDrunen's accessible, lucid book is the guide every Protestant needs to recover natural law today."

—**Matthew Barrett**, professor of Christian theology,
Midwestern Baptist Theological Seminary

"*Natural Law: A Short Companion* is the finest introduction to
natural law for Reformed and evangelical Christians I have ever
encountered. Not only does it provide an insightful account of
what natural law is and where it comes from; it is also wonderfully
pastoral in its explanation of how the natural law is important to
discipleship and engagement with others."

—**William S. Brewbaker III**, William Alfred Rose
Professor of Law, University of Alabama School of Law

"Christians know the Ten Commandments but might be surprised
to discover that God has also written his law in creation and upon
the hearts of all human beings. Such an idea is neither human
invention nor merely church tradition but a scriptural truth that
VanDrunen explains with clarity, concision, and conviction. He
ably shows natural law's biblical foundations, theological characteristics, and connections to everyday life. Christians who want a
deeper understanding of what the Bible has to say about natural law
will benefit from this book."

—**J. V. Fesko**, Harriet Barbour Professor of Systematic and
Historical Theology, Reformed Theological Seminary

"David VanDrunen's academic work in the Reformed natural law tradition has already enriched the field of Christian ethics. In this short volume, he builds on his scholarly work to present an intellectually rich yet broadly accessible description of the scriptural and theological roots and contemporary application of the Reformed natural law tradition. He then moves natural law from the arena of the theoretical to expand upon its potential application for humble and faithful Christian engagement in the public square."

—**Elisabeth Rain Kincaid**, director of the Center for Ethics and Economic Justice, Loyola University

"David VanDrunen's latest book is a superb resource. He thoroughly demonstrates the biblical foundation for natural law. The clarity of VanDrunen's writing and argument is unexcelled. Placing natural law in the biblical category of wisdom disarms those disposed to rejecting natural law for its supposedly rationalistic character. VanDrunen's book should be read and studied by all who wish to understand how the ways of moral judgment are known to all—sinners and saints alike."

—**C. Scott Pryor**, professor of law, Campbell University

"In *Natural Law*, VanDrunen shows that a biblically faithful Protestant approach to ethics includes affirmation of the biblical concept of natural law. Some Christians who love the Scriptures wonder whether natural law is compatible with the Protestant faith, but in VanDrunen, we have an author whose commitment to the truth of Scripture leads him to defend it as a biblical concept. While brief, this book covers much ground, providing a helpful introduction to natural law while showing what we can learn about natural law through careful study of Scripture."

—**William Reddinger**, associate professor of government and criminal justice, Regent University

"*Natural Law* is another contribution by VanDrunen to the broader project of rehabilitating natural law for Protestant social ethics. In this work, VanDrunen has shown how intricately natural law principles are woven into the very fabric of the biblical story line. As the book's argument makes clear, there is no reason for evangelicals to remain reticent about the natural law considering the plentiful biblical data supporting it. Clear and accessible, this volume will be a helpful primer to all who read it."

—**Andrew T. Walker**, associate professor of Christian ethics, The Southern Baptist Theological Seminary

NATURAL LAW

ESSENTIALS *in Christian Ethics*

NATURAL LAW

A Short Companion

David VanDrunen

editors
C. Ben Mitchell & Jason Thacker

ACADEMIC
BRENTWOOD, TENNESSEE

Published by B&H Academic
Brentwood, Tennessee

ISBN: 978-1-0877-7541-8

Dewey Decimal Classification: 241
Subject Heading: NATURAL LAW \ PROVIDENCE AND
GOVERNMENT OF GOD \ GOD

Cover design by Emily Keafer Lambright. Cover illustration
by J614/iStock.

Printed in the United States of America

28 27 26 25 24 23 BTH 1 2 3 4 5 6 7 8 9 10

CONTENTS

SERIES PREFACE

In 1876, German Lutheran theologian Christoph Ernst Luthardt eloquently illustrated the relationship between theology and ethics. He wrote, "God first loved us is the summary of Christian doctrine. We love Him is the summary of Christian morality."[1] The wedding of theology and ethics was later embraced by generations of theologians and ethicists, such as Protestant titans Herman Bavinck and Carl F. H. Henry,[2] who rightly understood the primacy of both theology and ethics in the Christian life. But at times in the recent history of the Protestant church, the study of ethics has been relegated to a mere application of theology and biblical studies rather than understood as a first-order discipline in rich partnership with the theological task.

The aim of the Christian ethic can be summed up in the words of Jesus in Matt 22:37–39. We, God's people, are to "love the Lord

---

[1] Christoph Ernst Luthardt, *Apologetic Lectures on the Moral Truths of Christianity*, trans. Sophia Taylor (Edinburgh: T&T Clark, 1876), 26.

[2] See Herman Bavinck, *Reformed Ethics*. ed. John Bolt, vol. 1, *Created, Fallen, and Converted Humanity* (Grand Rapids: Baker, 2019), §1:58; and Carl F. H. Henry, *Christian Personal Ethics*, 2nd ed. (Grand Rapids: Baker, 1979), 486.

[our] God with all [our] heart[s] and with all [our] soul[s] and with all [our] mind[s] . . . and to love [our] neighbor as [ourselves]." We hear echoes of this summation in the words of Luthardt, Bavinck, and Henry, each of whom spoke of how God's people are to love him as the summary of Christian morality. Thus, Christian ethics is nothing less than a primary motivation for those seeking to be faithful to God in all of life and live in light of how he has revealed himself in Scripture. Ethics as discipleship is a key theme throughout Scripture and one the church must elevate as we seek God's face in the academy, in our churches, and especially in our personal lives as transformed creatures made in the very image of God.

While Christian ethics is a core element of God's revelation to his people about how they are to live as his followers, it is also a distinct philosophical discipline that must be studied in consideration of the rich history of moral thought seen throughout the life of the church and the wider society. Much of today's discourse about Christian ethics tends to focus on the mere application of theological or philosophical principles, rather than on understanding how these principles have been derived and refined over time in light of the massive metaphysical and epistemological shifts in the history of thought.

Given the recent tendency in wider evangelicalism at times to downplay the direct study of ethics in our curricula, in our church life, and in the task of discipleship, the Essentials in Christian Ethics series is designed to illuminate the richness of the Christian ethic, as well as how ethics is intricately woven into the whole of the Christian life. We have gathered renowned ethicists and leading figures in their fields of theological and philosophical inquiry who are passionate about proclaiming the biblical ethic to a world desperately in need of Christ.

The series is made up of short, introductory volumes spanning metaethics, normative ethics, and applied ethics. Each volume can be used independently as an introduction to the crucial elements of the Christian ethical tradition, including resources for further reading and key concepts for those seeking to dig deeper into the beauty of God's revelation. They can also be used as supplements to a larger ethics curriculum, where a specialized volume could be used to augment a primary text or to give deeper insight into particular contemporary ethical debates.

As editors, we have longed for a series like this to be written by scholars who understand and apply the rich relationship of theology and ethics in their teaching, writings, and ministry. This series is designed to model for readers how the biblical ethic applies to every area of life both as a distinct theological and a philosophical discipline in the context of the Christian moral tradition from a robust Protestant viewpoint. We pray this serves the wider academy, those training in our colleges and seminaries, and especially those seeking to employ the riches of Christian ethics in the context of the local church.

C. Ben Mitchell and Jason Thacker
Series Editors

ACKNOWLEDGMENTS

I am grateful to Jason Thacker and Ben Mitchell for inviting me to write this book. Between 2010 and 2020, I published three large academic volumes on natural law that developed my thoughts on this topic in considerable detail. The new book has provided an opportunity to present the results of my research and reflection in a concise and (I hope) accessible way. But readers interested in exploring subjects covered in this book in more detail may wish to consult those earlier volumes. Thus, I have included footnotes that will direct you to where you may find these more detailed discussions. The following acronyms refer to these books: NLTK = *Natural Law and the Two Kingdoms*; DCMO = *Divine Covenants and Moral Order*; and PAC = *Politics after Christendom.*[1] I have also made a few references to a future book of mine in which I'll also

[1] *Natural Law and the Two Kingdoms: A Study in the Development of Reformed Social Thought* (Grand Rapids: Eerdmans, 2010); *Divine Covenants and Moral Order: A Biblical Theology of Natural Law* (Grand Rapids: Eerdmans, 2014); and *Politics after Christendom: Political Theology in a Fractured World* (Grand Rapids: Zondervan Academic, 2020). I also wrote a short introduction to natural law almost twenty years ago, *before* writing any of these three academic books: *A Biblical Case for Natural Law* (Grand Rapids: Acton Institute, 2006). I have learned a great deal since

provide more detailed discussion of some issues considered in the present book: RMT = *Reformed Moral Theology.*[2]

I wish to thank my son Jack for reading this manuscript and for his helpful feedback.

---

writing that book, and I believe the present work offers a better and more mature introduction to the topic.

[2] *Reformed Moral Theology: Law, Virtue, and Spirituality* (Grand Rapids: Baker Academic, forthcoming).

1

Introduction to Natural Law

Natural law refers to *the law of God made known in the created order, which all human beings know through their physical senses, intellect, and conscience, although they sinfully resist this knowledge to various degrees.* Understood in this way, natural law is an essential part of Christian theology and ethics. Without natural law, Christianity would not make sense. The nonexistence of natural law would throw Christian claims about God, the gospel, and the moral life into disarray. Perhaps these seem like exaggerated or overly dramatic claims. This book as a whole will explain and defend them but will consider a few things initially.

One of Christianity's great confessions about God is that he is judge of all the world and his judgments are righteous and just. If true, several other truths must follow. God must be omniscient, for example, knowing all relevant facts about every person's life. God must be omnipotent as well, able to summon everyone before his heavenly tribunal and overcome all opposition. It is also necessary that all people genuinely understand their responsibilities toward God. God would not be just if he judged people for actions they had no way of knowing were wrong. Some individuals have heard and read the Scriptures, and God can justly judge them for disobeying its commands. But what about the vast multitude of people throughout history who are completely ignorant of God's Word? On what basis will God judge them? Natural law is the law of God made known in creation to all people everywhere. They know it simply by virtue of being humans who live in this world. Natural law thus explains how God holds the whole world accountable to him. Without natural law, God would have no just basis for doing so.

Or consider a related issue at the heart of Christianity. The gospel of Jesus Christ proclaims salvation for sinners, accomplished by Christ's life, death, and resurrection and received through faith in him. While this gospel message is distinct from God's law—since the law tells us what God requires *of* us and the gospel announces what God has done *for* us—the gospel makes no sense without the law. If God's law did not alert people to their disobedience and condemn them under God's judgment, they would not need salvation or a gospel message. Yet Christianity insists that the gospel is good news for all, relevant and understandable to people everywhere (e.g., Rom 1:16). This is precisely why the church sends missionaries to places where the Scriptures are not yet known. But this assumes that people in such places are *already* lost and condemned before God. God's law must already have come to them even before Scripture has. The only law this could be is the natural law. The natural law explains why the gospel is relevant and intelligible to all people.

Without the reality of natural law, furthermore, Christians would be unable to explain the way they think about moral life in the world. For instance, Christians believe they should support what is just. They also know that justice is not simply what governments say is just. Government officials are often the worst perpetrators of injustice, and thus promoting justice may require holding them to account. We might think of notorious examples in which tyrants have been brought before international tribunals to face charges of genocide, war crimes, or crimes against humanity. Yet on what basis can officials from one country prosecute officials from another, as happened with Nazis at the Nuremberg trials? According to what law can they make their judgments if these tyrants have in fact followed the official "law" of their own countries? Everything depends on the reality of a law that ought to underlie all civil laws, a law that all people are obligated to obey even if their societies' "laws" direct them otherwise. What law could this be but the natural law?

On a more mundane level, Christians are part of civil communities and believe they should seek the peace and welfare of those communities (Jer 29:7). Christ has not given his people the sword to impose Christianity by force, so they must live and work alongside and collaborate with unbelievers to promote what is good. Even if their neighbors do not believe the gospel, Christians still care about how these neighbors conduct themselves in earthly affairs. Christians do not think their unbelieving neighbors should be baptized or participate in the Lord's Supper, but they do think they should work rather than steal, get married rather than cohabitate, bear and raise children rather than abort them, and vote for good candidates rather than bad ones. But how can Christians have meaningful moral conversations with non-Christians about such things? If Christians only appeal to Bible verses to try to persuade their non-Christian neighbors, they communicate a not-so-subtle hint that such moral issues are simply *Christian* things, things our holy book tells us to do. But work, marriage, and child-rearing are not simply Christian things, but *human* things. They concern matters that obligate all human beings and that have profound effect on the health of earthly communities. Without natural law, we could not explain why these moral issues concern all members of our societies and not just Christians who read about these issues in Scripture. The reality of natural law creates the possibility of Christians making moral appeals to their unbelieving neighbors in ways other than simply quoting the Bible.

The Plan of This Book

We will consider all of these issues in more detail in the pages to come. But I hope this opening discussion has provided a sense of why natural law is important for Christian theology and ethics. The book in your hands aims to offer an introduction to this interesting and practical topic.

I have written this volume primarily for Christians, to help them understand what natural law is and why it is important. It does not try to persuade non-Christians that there is a natural law or to change their minds about any particular moral issue, although perhaps some non-Christians will be interested in reading this book to learn what Christians think about natural law. I should also clarify that this is not an instruction manual giving Christians tips for making brilliant arguments that will stump people who hold bad moral views. Any book that claims to do that is probably making false promises. We will spend some time reflecting on Christian engagement with the public square through natural law, which is indeed an important topic, but we should beware of reducing natural law to a quick and easy tool to make people look good in debates.

Instead, we will focus on what Scripture itself teaches about natural law. The entire canon of Scripture is true and authoritative, and this book treats it as such. Scripture never uses the term "natural law," but it repeatedly, in a variety of ways, refers to the reality of natural law or assumes its existence. The existence of natural law underlies what Scripture says about God's own nature, the cosmic order, the image of God, human community, the gospel of Christ, and the final judgment. Moreover, the story of Scripture from the original creation to the new creation would not hold together without natural law. This book hopes to help Christians understand this pivotal role of natural law in Scripture and God's government of the world. If it succeeds in this goal, you should come to know both the Bible and God better. Moreover, I hope you will better appreciate your place in your earthly communities and how God wishes you to live just and peaceful lives within them.

Chapter 2 explores how we live in an orderly and meaningful universe, despite postmodern claims to the contrary. Natural law is a central part of that order and meaning. Chapter 3 reflects on several biblical texts showing that knowledge of the natural law exists even in pagan civil communities—communities increasingly like our own. God uses this knowledge to restrain the full effects of sin and sustain a measure of justice and peace. Chapter 4 then considers God's justice in holding all human beings accountable to his judgment through their knowledge of the natural law. This knowledge also ensures that the gospel of Christ is relevant and understandable to everyone. In chapter 5, we will see that though Scripture is Christians' primary moral standard, living the Christian life is impossible without knowing the natural law as well. Finally, chapter 6 explores how we come to know what the natural law requires and what this means for Christian engagement with unbelievers in the public square.

In the remainder of this present chapter, I will clarify some aspects of natural law. I also wish to reassure readers who may

harbor lingering suspicions that believing in natural law might subtly betray their Christian convictions.

Natural Revelation and
Natural Law Theory

I have run into numerous people over the years who object to natural law not because they disagree with the idea this book is defend-
ing but because they think "natural law" refers to something else.
Of course, people might have legitimate disagreements about how
best to define "natural law," but we must be clear about the terms
we use. This section will thus clarify the relationship between *natural law* and *natural revelation* and then will distinguish *natural law*
from *natural law theory*.

First, then, I suggest that we understand natural law as *an
aspect* of natural revelation. People have told me on occasion that
they believe in natural revelation rather than natural law. As I have
understood them, they believe that God reveals his moral will in
nature but think that natural law is something different from this.
Yet I am suggesting that God's revelation of his moral will in nature
is exactly what natural law is. If we embrace the idea of natural
revelation as Scripture describes it, we also believe in natural law.

In general, natural revelation refers to God making truth
known through the created order. In *special revelation*, by contrast,
God has made truth known through miracles, prophetic words,
and Christ himself. Scripture was written by Spirit-inspired prophets and apostles, and thus it is an example of special revelation.
But Scripture itself acknowledges the existence of God's revelation
in nature. One famous example is Ps 19:1: "The heavens declare
the glory of God, and the sky above proclaims his handiwork."

Romans 1:18–32 is another. This text demonstrates why natural law is indeed an aspect of natural revelation.

Romans 1:18–32 identifies two things natural revelation makes known: God himself and what God requires of human beings. We see the first of these in the opening verses of the text. Paul wrote that "what can be known about God is plain to them" (1:19), that is, to the unrighteous people he had just mentioned (1:18). He explains that "God has shown it to them" (1:19) and that God's "invisible attributes, namely, his eternal power and divine nature, have been clearly perceived, ever since the creation of the world, in the things that have been made" (1:20). Paul also notes that although sinful humans have not honored or given thanks to him, they "knew God" (1:21). This means that knowledge of God's existence and character is not simply *possible* to know from observing and reflecting on the created order. People do know it. Because of this, Paul concludes that people "are without excuse" (1:20). This last statement indicates that natural revelation brings moral responsibilities: all people are obligated to honor and give thanks to God, and they know it. This moral dimension of natural revelation becomes even clearer in subsequent verses.

Paul mentions many sins, beginning with idolatry (1:22–23) and homosexual conduct (1:24–27) and culminating with a long list of various offenses (1:28–31). Paul then concludes, "Though they know God's righteous decree that those who practice such things deserve to die, they not only do them but give approval to those who practice them" (1:32). These people do not just *possibly* know things from natural revelation; they do know them. What they know is that those who commit the sins just named deserve to die under God's righteous judgment. Nevertheless, they keep doing these things and support others who do them.

So, we see that natural revelation, according to Romans 1, communicates two truths: knowledge of God himself and knowledge of God's moral requirements. Based simply on this text, we can see that natural revelation includes not only what is sometimes called *the natural knowledge of God* but also *natural law*. It is difficult to know why someone might object to using "law" to refer to God's moral requirements known through natural revelation. Romans 2 confirms that this is an appropriate term to use. In this text, Paul again discusses all people's accountability before God's judgment (2:12–16). He says that even Gentiles, who do not have God's written (biblical) law, "by nature do what the law requires" and "are a law to themselves." They "show that the work of the law is written on their hearts, while their conscience also bears witness, and their conflicting thoughts accuse or even excuse them" (2:14–15).

Why would anybody think that we must choose between natural revelation and natural law? A possible source of confusion is that many Christian theologians have associated natural law with human *reason*. One might have in mind statements by medieval theologian Thomas Aquinas. He said, for example, that by "the light of natural reason . . . we discern what is good and what is evil, which is the function of the natural law."[1] This statement may leave the impression that natural law is something our own reason proclaims, or even that reason itself *is* the natural law. But a much better way to understand this point (and more faithful to Aquinas's own view) is that reason is one of our human capacities *by which we understand* what the natural law is.

---

[1] *Summa Theologize* 1a2ae 91.2. English translations are taken from Thomas Aquinas, *Summa Theologica*, 5 vols., trans. Fathers of the English Dominican Province (Allen, TX: Christian Classics, 1981).

Our physical senses take in natural revelation, our reason reflects upon it, and our conscience makes judgments about it. Natural law is *God's*; reason is *ours*. God reveals his natural law to us, and our reason reflects upon it and comes to conclusions about it. In fact, reason plays a similar role with respect to *biblical* law. God reveals his law to us in Scripture, and our reason reflects upon it and interprets it.

This brings us to the second thing I wish to clarify in this section: the distinction between *natural law* and *natural law theory*. This distinction is quite close to the distinction I just made between natural law and reason.

Some people may be tempted to speak critically of natural law if they have been unconvinced by some writer's theory of natural law or have heard a speaker make a stupid-sounding "natural law argument." But doing so, whether intentionally or not, identifies natural law with what people say about it. This is a fundamental error. Just because a person tries to play a Chopin nocturne and does a terrible job does not make that nocturne a bad piece of music. Or to hit closer to home: just because a preacher misinterprets and misapplies a biblical text from the pulpit on Sunday does not mean there is a problem with the text. Just as we must distinguish pieces of music and biblical texts from those who try to play or preach them, so we must distinguish the natural law from any particular theory about it.

People can make embarrassing arguments from "natural law" and develop unconvincing natural-law theories. We should think critically about natural-law arguments and theories, but this does not imply that there is something wrong with natural law itself. Human reason is fallen and is always liable to error when it interprets God's revelation. We need to be careful not to criticize God's revelation because of our own sinful handling of it.

Natural Law, Rome, and
the Reformation

It seems wise to address another issue that weighs on many minds
when someone raises the issue of natural law: Is natural law a
Roman Catholic notion, and if so, must Protestants who embrace
natural law give up some of their theological convictions and accept
Roman Catholic views?

Absolutely not, although it is understandable that some readers
may have suspected otherwise. It is true, after all, that the Roman
Catholic tradition has consistently affirmed natural law and developed much of their ethical teaching through natural-law reasoning.
Furthermore, most twentieth-century Protestant theologians and
ethicists gave little attention to natural law, and often the attention
they did give it was negative. A person who picks up a few random
twentieth-century Roman Catholic ethical works and compares
them to a few random twentieth-century Protestant ethical works
may well get the impression that Roman Catholics get their ethics
from natural law and Protestants from Scripture.

A couple of valid theological concerns have also raised Protestant suspicions about natural law. For one thing, Roman Catholics
tend to have a less dire view of human sinfulness than Protestants
(or at least Protestants in the Reformed and Lutheran traditions).
Natural law theory, it may appear, depends on a naively optimistic
view of what human reason can figure out. If sinners are as fallen
as Scripture and Reformation theologians say they are, such optimism seems misplaced. Another theological concern is that Roman
Catholics do not affirm the doctrine of *sola scriptura*. If the Bible
is indeed sufficient, we might wonder whether ethical appeals to
natural law are necessary at all. Perhaps such appeals reflect a lack
of confidence in Scripture?

Shortly after the turn of the twenty-first century, there was a renaissance of interest in natural law among Protestants.[2] But even some of the Protestants who promoted this renaissance may have inadvertently reinforced the idea that natural law is a Roman Catholic idea. They did this by presenting natural law predominantly through discussing Roman Catholic writers and by suggesting, in effect, that Protestants should tag along and affirm natural law *despite* being Protestant.[3]

However, Protestants should not affirm natural law despite being Protestant. They should affirm natural law *because* they are Protestant.

This is true, first of all, because Scripture says so much about natural law. I have already discussed this briefly, and subsequent chapters will explore it more thoroughly. But the basic point here is this: Protestants believe that Scripture is the highest authority for Christian faith and life, and since Scripture clearly teaches the reality and importance of natural law, Protestants must affirm natural law if they wish to be true to their own convictions.

Another reason Protestants *as Protestants* should affirm natural law is because this is what Protestants have done historically. In the Reformation era, leading reformers appealed to natural law repeatedly. Martin Luther, for example, interpreted Paul's statement concerning "the work of the law" written on the heart

---

[2] Among the larger and earlier contributions, see NLTK; Stephen J. Grabill, *Rediscovering the Natural Law in Reformed Theological Ethics* (Grand Rapids: Eerdmans, 2006); J. Daryl Charles's *Retrieving the Natural Law: A Return to Moral First Things* (Grand Rapids: Eerdmans, 2008); and Robert C. Baker and Roland Cap Ehlke, eds., *Natural Law: A Lutheran Reappraisal* (St. Louis: Concordia, 2011).

[3] In my judgment, this is true of Charles's *Retrieving the Natural Law.*

(Rom 2:14–15) as a reference to natural law.[4] He also believed that natural law is summarized in the Ten Commandments.[5] Elsewhere he described natural law as a higher law than human legal systems.[6] Then he wrote that Christians should obey the law of Moses when it "agrees with both the New Testament and the natural law."[7] John Calvin's many comments on natural law express similar sentiments. When commenting on Rom 2:14–15, he wrote of God's law "imprinted" and "engraven" on the heart and will, which people know through their consciences.[8] He identified this implanted law with the "moral law" and the precepts of the Ten Commandments.[9] Calvin also taught that natural law should be the standard for all human civil law, though in a flexible manner appropriate to time and place.[10] Human legal systems should adhere to the natural law rather than to the judicial regulations of the Mosaic law.[11]

---

[4] E.g., see Martin Luther, "Lectures on Romans," in *Luther's Works*, vol. 25, ed. Hilton C. Oswald (St. Louis: Concordia, 1972), 186–87; and "Against the Heavenly Prophets in the Matter of Images and Sacraments," in *Luther's Works*, vol. 40, ed. Conrad Bergendoff (Philadelphia: Fortress, 1958), 97.

[5] E.g., see Luther, "Against the Heavenly Prophets," 98; and "How Christians Should Regard Moses," in *Luther's Works*, vol. 35, ed. E. Theodore Bachmann (Philadelphia: Fortress, 1960), 172–73.

[6] E.g., see Martin Luther, "Temporal Authority: To What Extent It Should Be Obeyed," in *Luther's Works*, vol. 45, ed. Walther I. Brandt (Philadelphia: Muhlenberg, 1962), 127–28.

[7] E.g., see Luther, "How Christians Should Regard Moses," 165.

[8] John Calvin, *Commentaries on the Epistle of Paul the Apostle to the Romans*, trans. and ed. John Owen (Edinburgh: Calvin Translation Society, 1849; Grand Rapids: Baker, 2003), 97–99.

[9] E.g., see John Calvin, *Institutes of the Christian Religion*, 1.3.1; 1.3.3; 2.2.14; 2.2.22; 2.8.1; 4.20.16.

[10] E.g., see Calvin, *Institutes*, 4.20.16.

[11] E.g., see Calvin, 4.20.14–16.

Later Protestant theologians advocated the same views, although they often explained them with more depth and precision. To give but one example, the prominent seventeenth-century Reformed scholastic theologian Francis Turretin argued that the natural law is "impressed by God upon the conscience of man." This law expresses "the difference between right and wrong" and contains "the practical principles of immovable truth." Turretin recognized that the testimony of natural law has been "corrupted and obscured by sin," but nevertheless "so many remains and evidences of this law are still left in our nature . . . that there is no mortal who cannot feel its force either more or less."[12] Natural law, for Turretin, is "the rule of justice and injustice," such that human legislators should put it into concrete legal form according to their discretion.[13] These legislators may impose the Mosaic judicial law only "inasmuch as it agrees with the natural law and is founded on it."[14]

Early Protestant theologians did not seem to regard natural law as especially controversial. This is not surprising in historical context, however. Long before the Reformation, natural law was a common topic in Christian thought. Important thinkers from the early church promoted the idea of natural law.[15] Even prominent medieval figures such as Thomas Aquinas, Duns Scotus, and William of Ockham, whose theologies differed in many important

---

[12] Francis Turretin, *Institutes of Elenctic Theology*, vol. 2, *Eleventh through Seventeenth Topics*, trans. George Musgrave Giger, ed. James T. Dennison Jr. (Phillipsburg, NJ: P&R, 1992), 3.

[13] Turretin, 2:2, 167.

[14] Turretin, 2:167.

[15] E.g., see Lactantius, *The Divine Institutes*, VI.8, in *The Fathers of the Church*, vol. 49, trans. Sister Mary Francis McDonald, OP (Washington, DC: The Catholic University of America Press, 1964), 411–13; and *The Etymologies of Isidore of Seville*, ed. Stephen A. Barney et al. (Cambridge: Cambridge University Press, 2008), 117 (V.ii–iv).

ways, agreed that natural law exists, that human beings are obligated to obey it, and that it provides the proper foundation for human civil law.[16] Since theologians had affirmed natural law for so long, early Protestants regarded it as a standard part of Christian theology and ethics. The reformers, of course, believed that many aspects of medieval theology required serious correction according to the Word of God, but they did not think that *all* doctrines required reformation. On key issues such as the Trinity, the divine attributes, and the two natures of Christ in one person, they recognized that medieval theologians held orthodox views in continuity with the early church and Scripture itself. The reformers had no interest in changing these doctrines. Natural law belongs in this category. Early Protestant theologians explained natural law in some of their own ways, but for the most part they simply affirmed what the church had already affirmed for a long time.

This should be encouraging for Protestants today. The reformers never saw themselves as founding a new church, but as *reforming* the one church of Christ that he promised to build and to protect from the assaults of hell (Matt 16:18–19). They loved to note how their theology agreed not only with Scripture but also with great theologians and ecclesiastical confessions throughout the history of the church. We who are Protestants should view patristic and medieval theology as part of *our own history*. When contemporary Protestants recognize natural law as part of their theology and ethics, they follow not only their own Protestant tradition but also the earlier tradition that preceded it, all the way back to Scripture.

But some readers may still wonder about the theological issues mentioned above. Does appealing to natural law not reflect too

---

[16] For discussion of these theologians' views and citation of their works on these points, see NLTK, 43–55.

optimistic a view of human sin and constitute a rejection of biblical sufficiency? A few words here may help to alleviate these legitimate concerns, and later parts of this book will address them in more detail.

First, the depth and deception of sin does indeed affect human beings' ability to understand natural law and put it into practice. But the natural world continues to declare God's glory and righteousness. Human rebellion does not change the fact that the natural law exists and that it impresses our obligations toward God and neighbor upon our hearts. Sinful people's response to natural law is complicated. Romans 1:18–32 teaches, on the one hand, that all people *know* God's existence and attributes through the created order (1:19–20) and *know* that those who commit a long list of sins deserve to die (1:28–32). On the other hand, sinful people resist this natural knowledge of God (1:18, 21) and continue to practice sins worthy of death (1:32). What Romans 1 says matches our experience in the world: fallen humans do many noble and productive things but also many terrible and destructive things. They show that they continue to be divine image-bearers who know God's law and simultaneously show the corruption sin has worked in their lives.

This requires a balanced presentation of natural law. We should not underestimate how God's mysterious providence governs this sinful world and uses the testimony of natural law to promote much that is good in our societies. But we do not want to be naively optimistic about what we can accomplish by dazzling people with natural-law arguments about controversial moral issues. Our study of Scripture in the following chapters will reinforce both of these points.

Second, affirming the importance of natural law is not at odds with the Reformation notion of *sola scriptura* (Scripture alone). *Sola scriptura* does not mean that the Bible provides answers to every question, and it does not eliminate the need for other sources of knowledge. Traditionally, *sola scriptura* means that Scripture is the sufficient source of *special revelation*. In other words, Christians do not need new inspired words from God—either from prophets, apostles, or the pope in Rome.[17] Scripture is Christians' highest standard and only infallible authority. *Sola scriptura* does not mean, however, that *natural revelation* is unnecessary. To claim such would be absurd. Scripture itself presumes that we know all sorts of things about the world in which we live.[18] It refers to the sun, moon, and stars; to birds, fish, and horses; to Egypt, Babylon, and the Jordan River. Without natural revelation, we would not know what any of these things are, and Scripture would make no sense to us. Moreover, Scripture directs its readers to learn about the moral life from the natural world. Proverbs, for instance, speaks of the created order as the product of God's wisdom (8:22–31) and instructs us to go to the ant to become wise (6:6–11).

A high view of Scripture, therefore, should make us all the more attentive to the natural world and eager to learn and follow the natural law. We are now ready to pursue that goal in the chapters ahead.

---

[17] As the Westminster Confession of Faith puts it when describing biblical sufficiency, nothing is to be added to Scripture "whether by new revelations of the Spirit, or traditions of men" (1.6).

[18] Cf. Matthew Barrett, *God's Word Alone: The Authority of Scripture* (Grand Rapids: Zondervan, 2016), 337–39.

2

A Meaningful and Purposeful World

As argued in the previous chapter, natural law refers to the revelation of God's moral will for human beings through the natural created order. If such a natural law exists, it tells us something about the world we inhabit. The world must be meaningful and purposeful, and we must be the kind of creatures who can grasp this meaning and purpose. It seems highly unlikely that a random and chaotic world could communicate anything understandable about the proper way to live.

But what sort of world do we live in? That is a controversial question today. It would have been much less controversial for the medieval and Reformation-era theologians who wrote about natural law. They believed that God created the world, instilled it with meaning and purpose, and made human beings capable of understanding it. For them, the world has meaning and purpose (whether we acknowledge it or not), and it is our responsibility as humans to discover its truth and live accordingly. They lived in a so-called *premodern* culture.

Cultural assumptions about the world changed with the rise of *modernity*, often associated with the European Enlightenment of the eighteenth century. Many proponents of this movement became skeptical that the world has meaning and purpose. And even if the world does have meaning, these thinkers did not think humans are able to perceive it. For them, human beings do not *discover* meaning in the world but *project* or *impose* meaning onto it. Many writers continued to speak about natural law in early modernity, but it was a stripped-down version. They believed that if we all act rationally, we will all impose the same sort of meaning onto the world. Thus, they held out hope for a universal human ethics based on reason.[1]

But assumptions shifted again with the rise of so-called *postmodernism* over the past century. Postmodern culture not only lacks confidence that the world is inherently meaningful but also questions the reality of universal human reason. In postmodern perspective, each individual or community imposes *its own* meaning on the world. There is no generic human rationality that can judge whether anyone's meaning is good or bad. This is why we hear so much about tolerance in our day (inconsistent as that tolerance may be). If there is no meaning or purpose to the world and no rationality we all share, then it makes sense that we should tolerate and even celebrate the way individuals and communities choose to

---

[1] Immanuel Kant, for example, expressed many of these sentiments. See his *Groundwork for the Metaphysics of Morals*, ed. Allen W. Wood (New Haven: Yale University Press, 2002). On natural law among Enlightenment thinkers, see especially Knud Haakonssen, *Natural Law and Moral Philosophy: From Grotius to the Scottish Enlightenment* (Cambridge: Cambridge University Press, 1996).

live. This context also explains the rise of identity politics. When people are left to create their own meaning, they naturally gravitate toward people who create meaning in similar ways and thus they group together to find their identity. But as time goes by, the number of such groups tends to multiply, and social cohesion becomes increasingly strained.

Evolutionary philosophy also contributes to the contemporary loss of confidence in a meaningful world. I do not refer to the general idea that there is evolution in nature (which there clearly is) but to the larger philosophical idea that this world has always been in a state of purposeless evolutionary flux. In the predominant Darwinian scheme, the world is not evolving *toward* something or under the guidance of any supernatural person or force.[2] Evolution is random and has no goal.

In such a context, it is no surprise that appeals to natural law often meet with puzzlement or hostility. Yet people are still looking for meaning in their lives and feel despair when they lack it. This would be hard to explain if the world were not meaningful: Why would meaningless beings in a meaningless universe be so obsessed with the meaning of life? This longing for meaning unlocks ways for the natural law to do its work, however subtly. It also opens up possible lines of communication between those who still believe in a meaningful world and those who (think they) do not.

It is appropriate that we consider such issues early in the book. This chapter, therefore, begins by reflecting on God's creation of the world. We will see, especially from Genesis 1 and Proverbs 8, that God indeed made this world meaningful and purposeful and made his image-bearers fit to understand it. We will then reflect on

---

[2] See for example Ernst Mayr, *What Evolution Is* (New York: Basic, 2001), 75–76.

how Scripture describes our fallen world and observe how meaning and purpose endure, despite the corruption of sin. The chapter concludes by exploring some easily overlooked biblical texts that point to the meaningfulness of the world and provide further evidence for the natural law.

The Original Created Order

Genesis 1 is the obvious place to begin. Three matters seem especially important to note: how God put everything in its proper place, how he created things with functions to perform, and how he made all things good. Let's consider these first as regards the nonhuman creation.

At every step along the way, Genesis 1 describes God putting everything in just the right place. God created a world that is perfectly orderly. We see first that God made the light and separated it from the darkness (1:4), and later that he created the heavenly lights to do this work of separation (1:14–15, 17). Light and darkness had their own place in God's order. So, too, with the waters above and the waters below, for God created "an expanse" to separate them from each other (1:6–7). God also gathered the waters below into one place, to distinguish them from the dry ground (1:9). The expanse, the seas, and the land all had their proper place, and each of them provided the proper dwelling for certain kinds of living creatures. God made the sea creatures for the water, the birds for the heavenly expanse (1:20–21), and the livestock and beasts for the land (1:24–25). Nothing was random or arbitrary. God situated everything right where he wanted it. The text reinforces this by saying that God created the various living things "according to their kinds" (1:11, 21, 24–25). The types of creatures and their interrelations exist according to God's master plan.

God gave his creatures jobs to do within this perfect order. Hence, created things exist for a purpose. We see this first with the expanse: "Let it separate the waters from the waters" (1:6). Likewise with the dry land, which God made to "sprout vegetation" (1:11–12), and with the lights in the expanse, which were "to separate the day from the night," to be signs for the passage of time, to give light on earth, and to rule over day and night (1:14–18). The sea and the land also had tasks: to swarm with fish (1:20–21) and to bring forth living creatures of the earth (1:24). God did not exactly give these creatures *moral responsibilities* since they lack reason and thus cannot obey God voluntarily. They obey him necessarily. But these various statements indicate that the world is thoroughly purposeful. Things exist for a reason, to fulfill God's brilliant plan.

Perhaps it goes without saying that if God put everything in its rightful place, with its proper job, the natural order must be supremely excellent. But the text leaves no question about it: while recounting the creation of nonhuman creatures, it tells us six times that God looked at what he had made and "saw that it was good" (1:4, 10, 12, 18, 21, 25). God himself is good, and his handiwork reflects and embodies that goodness.

The same is true for God's creation of human beings—in enhanced fashion. God put them in their proper place (that is, the earth) (1:28), which they shared with land animals. Yet God did not make them according to *their own* kind but "in *our* image, after *our* likeness" (1:26): "in the image of God he created . . . them" (1:27). We belong in this world to reflect God's glory in special measure (cf. Ps 8:5). God also gave humans a job to do. He created them as image-bearers for a purpose: to "have dominion" over the other creatures and to be fruitful, multiply, fill the earth, and subdue it (Gen 1:26, 28). This was a *moral* commission. Humans alone had the ability to obey it, especially due to their intellectual and spiritual gifts. Finally, God's creation of humans was supremely excellent. After God made them, and thus finished creation in its entirety, he "saw everything that he had made, and behold, it was very good" (1:31).

Proverbs describes the purposeful order of creation from another angle: God made all things *through wisdom*. Proverbs first says this in 3:19–20: "The LORD by wisdom founded the earth; by understanding he established the heavens; by his knowledge the deeps broke open, and the clouds drop down the dew." A little later, 8:22–31 provides a creation account as powerful and beautiful as Genesis 1. It depicts wisdom as a woman. God brought forth wisdom before creation and possessed her at the outset of his work (8:22–26). The text describes God's formation of the heavens, the skies, the sea, and the earth (8:27–29). All along, wisdom "was there" (8:27) and "beside him, like a master workman" (8:30). Wisdom was God's own delight (8:30), and wisdom in turn rejoiced in the world and delighted in human beings (8:31). A world so thoroughly saturated with divine wisdom can hardly be chaotic and random. Instead, the created order overflows with meaning and purpose that reflects God's infinite understanding. Such a world must indeed be very good.

To return to Genesis: The opening chapters of Scripture communicate that God made human beings intimately part of this natural world. In many respects we are like the animals: Genesis calls nonhuman animals "living creatures" (1:20, 21, 24), and it also calls the first man a "living creature" (2:7). We are made of the earth's stuff: as God made the land animals from "the earth" (1:24), so he formed the first man "of dust from the ground" (2:7). God also called humans to fill and subdue the earth (1:28), to eat the plants (1:29), and to rule the animals (1:26). In all these things we see that God made us to fit in this world, to be able to understand it, and to be at home there.

Even while thoroughly a part of the natural world, humans also resemble God. Many Christian theologians have speculated on what exactly makes us God's image. They have suggested it is because we have a soul, or reason, or will. It is difficult to imagine how we would be image-bearers without having such things, but Genesis 1 highlights something else: God has *called us to work*. He made us in his image and likeness *so that* we might have dominion over the other creatures (1:26). To be an image-bearer is to be called to this great task. It is to have a moral commission.[3] As God worked supremely in creating and ordering this world, so he made humans to rule and subdue it further under his ultimate authority.

This has profound implications for how we think about human nature. There are many things we can say about our nature, but one essential aspect is that humans bear God's image. The image of God is *who we are*. And to be God's image means to have a moral calling in this world. Thus, who we *are* and what we are *called to do* are inseparable. To know human nature is to know something about human moral responsibilities. And those human moral responsibilities would hardly have seemed strange to our first parents. God

---

[3] On reading Gen 1:26 as containing a purpose clause, see, for example, Paul Joüon, S.J., *A Grammar of Biblical Hebrew*, trans. and rev. T. Muraoka (Rome: Editrice Pontifecio Instituto Biblico, 1991), 2:381. On the moral commission as part of the image itself, see e.g., D. J. A. Clines, "Humanity as the Image of God," in *On the Way to the Postmodern: Old Testament Essays, 1967–1998*, vol. 2, ed. D. J. A. Clines (Sheffield, UK: Sheffield Academic, 1998), 490–92; and J. Richard Middleton, *The Liberating Image: The* Imago Dei *in Genesis 1* (Grand Rapids: Brazos, 2005), 53–54.

called them to act in, with, and upon this natural world, and he
made them an intimate part of this world, perfectly equipped to do
what his image entailed.

These considerations provide a response to a common objection to natural law, i.e., that natural law falls prey to the so-called
is-ought problem.[4] According to this objection, nature tells us
what is. Different things have different characteristics that we can
identify and describe. But just because we know a thing's nature
does not mean we know what it ought to do. By nature, humans
have legs that are capable of walking. But this does not imply that
we ought to walk, for by the same reasoning we could say that
our legs are also capable of kicking people in the shins, and thus
we ought to do that. Along similar lines, perhaps you have heard
someone say: "The animals on my family's farm are heterosexual.
Homosexuality is thus contrary to nature, and it is immoral for
people to engage in it." By this same reasoning, one might also say,
"Bears hibernate in the winter. Thus, hibernating is natural, and
we ought to do so."

This is-ought objection does expose the fallacy of some "natural law" arguments. The fact that legs are capable of a variety of
movements does not prove anything about what movements they
ought to make and when to make them. The fact that pigs in the
barn and bears in the woods do certain things does not mean we
ought to imitate them. But this objection really does not hit home

---

[4] Scottish philosopher David Hume (1711–76) is usually credited
with identifying the is-ought problem in his work *A Treatise of Human
Nature*, 3.1.1. For a brief introduction to this and related ideas, see
e.g., Roger Crisp, "Fact/Value Distinction," in *Routledge Encyclopedia
of Philosophy*, vol. 3, ed. Edward Craig (New York: Routledge, 1998),
537–38.

against natural law as traditionally understood by Christians, or as defended in this book.

That is because the is-ought problem only makes sense if one thinks of nature in a modern or postmodern way. If nature has no meaning or purpose (postmodernism) or we cannot know what it is (modernism), then of course we cannot move logically from a description of nature to conclusions about how we ought to act. In such thinking, the sciences provide many facts about how nature works, which can be useful, but they remain simply facts. Meaning and lifestyle are ours to choose. But if nature is what Scripture says it is—a meaningful and purposeful created order—then we cannot simply separate *is* from *ought*. What is human nature? Human nature involves having two eyes, two ears, two kidneys, one nose, and one mouth. It involves having legs that can walk and kick. It requires eating, drinking, and sleeping. We know all of this from common observation, and science tells us other interesting details about our circulatory system, genetic code, and many more things. But this hardly exhausts human nature. To be human is to be God's image-bearer, which means having a moral commission (Gen 1:26) to be pursued in knowledge, righteousness, and holiness (Eph 4:24; Col 3:10). Thus, we cannot truly understand human nature without understanding how we should live. God made us for a purpose. He has given meaning to our existence. What we ought to do is wrapped up in what we are.

Keeping this in mind does mean that making "natural-law arguments" will be considerably more difficult than if we could simply deduce moral conclusions from facts we observe in nature. But it will also save us the embarrassment of making bad arguments. Chapter 6 will reflect on the challenging question of how Christians can engage others through natural law with theological integrity.

The Fallen Created Order

We have focused thus far on biblical texts that describe the original creation. Perhaps we are not surprised to see meaning, purpose, and order in the perfect cosmos God made, but we wonder if these things are still true following the entrance of evil into the world. Scripture not only speaks repeatedly of human sin but also says that God cursed the broader natural order (Gen 3:17–18; Rom 8:20–22). Can we still describe the world as meaningful, purposeful, and orderly? We are primarily interested in natural law here and now, not in some distant past, so these are serious issues to consider.

The rest of this chapter describes how Scripture does in fact see purpose, meaning, and order in the world after the fall. Scripture depicts humans as still fit for life in this world and equipped to gain moral knowledge from creation. The corruption of sin is indeed profound, but it has not annihilated the fundamental goodness of what God made. A holistically biblical account of the fallen world must affirm both the depth of evil and God's ongoing testimony to his righteousness and glory within the natural order. We see this first and foundationally in the account of the Noahic covenant after the great flood (Gen 8:21–9:17), although several subsequent texts provide powerful confirmation.

The Noahic Covenant

While God did not pledge to maintain order in the fallen world until after the great flood in Genesis 8–9, even the story of the fall in Genesis 3 suggests that the first sin did not cast creation into utter disorder. God pronounced a curse against the woman and man: women will have great pain in childbearing (3:16), relationships between husbands and wives will be strained (3:16), and men will gather food from the ground only through hard toil (3:17–19). Yet these curses communicate a subtle blessing too: there will still be childbearing, marriage, work, and food. The original created order was evidently corrupted, but not destroyed. The purposes of human existence described in Gen 1:26–29 have survived, although in tragic form.

Genesis 4 presents a tantalizingly brief history of human society between fall and flood. It makes life sound awful in many ways. It recounts multiple murders and boastful pride. But it also records marriages and childbirth and notes the development of agriculture, music, and metallurgy—from the ungodly line of Cain, no less. Genesis 4 leaves clear hints that order remains in the world and that fallen humans are capable of understanding it and producing useful and beautiful things from it.

Then God could put up with human violence no longer and brought the great flood (Genesis 6–7). Here the natural order did suddenly disintegrate. God dissolved the boundaries between different parts of creation that he had established in Genesis 1: "All the fountains of the great deep burst forth, and the windows of the heavens were opened," and "rain fell upon the earth forty days and forty nights" (7:11–12). God undid his work of gathering the sea into one place so that dry land could appear. The expanse in the heavens ceased to separate the waters above from the waters below. The consequence was predictable. Since the expanse and the dry land provided a home for birds, land animals, and human beings (1:20–21, 24–25, 28), when God dissolved the boundaries, "all flesh died that moved on the earth, birds, livestock, beasts, all swarming creatures that swarm on the earth, and all mankind" (7:21). The earth apparently reverted to being "without form and void" (1:2).

But things turned suddenly again when God "remembered Noah" and the creatures with him in the ark (8:1). "The fountains of the deep and the windows of the heavens were closed, the rain from the heavens was restrained, and the waters receded from the earth continually" (8:2–3), and finally dry land reappeared (8:4–5). God reestablished the boundaries that distinguished the heavens, earth, and sea. After the earth dried (8:13–14), Noah, his family, and their animal companions left the ark (8:15–16, 18–19). The animals could again do on earth what God made them to do in the beginning: to creep, swarm, be fruitful, and multiply (8:17; cf. 1:22, 24–25). The earth was again a fit home for God's creatures. He had reestablished order and purpose, and it resembled the original version.

But would this renewed order last? Yes. After Noah offered a sacrifice of thanksgiving to God (8:20), God entered a covenant with Noah, all his descendants, every living creature, and the earth (8:21–9:17). This was truly a universal covenant. God promised to maintain proper boundaries in the world: he would never again destroy the earth with a flood (9:11, 15), and thus the boundary between land and sea would endure. When rain comes, it will stop, as the sign of the rainbow testifies (9:13–14), indicating that the expanse would maintain the distinction between the waters above and below. God even put the fear of humans into the animals (9:2), thereby reasserting the clear difference between them that his original order required. God also promised order in the celestial bodies and the cycles of nature: "While the earth remains, seedtime and harvest, cold and heat, summer and winter, day and night, shall not cease" (8:22). This last statement helpfully informs us how long this covenant will be in effect: for as long as the present world endures.[5]

---

[5] It may be confusing, then, to see that the text later calls this covenant "everlasting" (9:16). The simple explanation is that the Hebrew term translated as "everlasting" can refer to a very long time without implying no end whatsoever. This is clearly the meaning here.

This means that it is still in effect today and will be until Christ returns.

Last but certainly not least, the Noahic covenant also calls "man" the "image" of God (9:6). We might be excused for wondering whether sinful humans, described as so violent and proud in Genesis 4 and 6, could still bear God's image. Up to this point Scripture has been silent on the issue. The account of the Noahic covenant begins by acknowledging man's deep-rooted sinfulness: "the intention of man's heart is evil from his youth" (8:21). But later it mentions the image of God: "Whoever sheds the blood of man, by man shall his blood be shed, for God made man in his image" (9:6). Thus, God prescribes blood-for-blood *because* he made humans his image-bearers. What's the logic behind this claim? The common interpretation is that murder deserves the most severe punishment because murder destroys someone with so much dignity, one who bears God's image. Another (and in my judgment more likely) interpretation is that this verse explains why *humans themselves* should take responsibility and avenge violence: they are divine image-bearers, created to rule in this world, and thus they should enforce justice.[6] Both interpretations only make sense if humans continue to be the image of God.

As we would expect if humans remain image-bearers, this covenant gives them moral responsibilities that resemble those of Gen 1:26–28. Not only should they do justice in response to violence (9:6), which seems appropriate for those whom God made rulers

---

[6] For one example of what I call the common interpretation, see Gordon J. Wenham, *Genesis 1–15* vol. 1 of *Word Biblical Commentary* (Waco, TX: Word, 1987), 193–94. For one example of the view that I regard as more likely, see W. Randall Garr, *In His Own Image and Likeness: Humanity, Divinity, and Monotheism* (Leiden: Brill, 2003), 163.

of creation (1:26), but they should also be fruitful, multiply, and fill the earth (9:1, 7), which repeats the original command of 1:28.

The Noahic covenant did not make all things right with the world. It assumes that evil continues to plague creation, and it makes no promise of salvation from sin or of everlasting life. But it does put a check on evil for the rest of world history. It maintains order in this world and treats human beings as divine image-bearers who live in this world for a purpose: to fill it and maintain justice within their societies. The fallen world fell into chaos during the great flood. But the Noahic covenant ensures that such chaos will not prevail again. And human beings have a divinely granted home and role within it.

The Natural Wisdom of Proverbs

Proverbs confirms the preceding interpretation of the Noahic covenant. Proverbs communicates that meaning, purpose, and order remain in our fallen world and that sinful humans are able to discern these things. To see this, we will revisit and expand our earlier study of Proverbs 8.

Proverbs 8:22–31 teaches that God created the world through wisdom, which means the created order could hardly be chaotic or meaningless. Or at least this is true of the *original* created order. The careful reader will notice that 8:22–31 only speaks about God's creative activity and says nothing about how God governs the world after the fall. Nevertheless, reading 8:22–31 in its larger context demonstrates that the meaning and order of the original creation must still exist in the present world.

In the immediately following verses, wisdom continues her speech begun in 8:22–31. Here, Wisdom makes an appeal to the readers of Proverbs: "And now, O sons, listen to me: blessed are those who keep my ways. Hear instruction and be wise, and do not neglect it. Blessed is the one who listens to me, watching daily at my gates, waiting beside my doors. For whoever finds me finds life and obtains favor from the LORD, but he who fails to find me injures himself; all who hate me love death" (8:32–36). This is fascinating to think about. The same wisdom the Lord possessed when he began to create and that accompanied him throughout this work is also accessible to human beings. God ordered the world through wisdom, and humans should live by wisdom too. This would be striking enough if the text were talking to Adam before the fall, but how much more remarkable that it addresses *sinners* instead. The divine wisdom reflected in the natural order is still available to people today.

When reading this text, however, we might wonder whether wisdom is really offered *within* and *through* the natural order. Could it be that Proverbs 8 calls us to seek God's creative wisdom, but we can only find it somewhere other than in creation? No, that is not what Proverbs teaches. It is true that Scripture elsewhere speaks about other ways to gain wisdom, such as through keeping God's law (Deut 4:6) and praying for wisdom (Jas 1:5). Proverbs does not deny the importance of such activities, but it says little about them. Proverbs emphasizes other things. One is that we gain wisdom by humbly heeding the advice and instruction of others, especially of parents and older people (e.g., 1:8; 10:17). Another is that we attain wisdom through observing the world around us, reflecting upon it, and coming to appropriate conclusions.

Proverbs describes this process of attaining wisdom in a variety of ways. People gain wisdom, for example, by observing human interaction and perceiving what sorts of results follow from which sorts of actions. A person can watch a young man seduced by a promiscuous woman, see what disaster it brings him, and learn

a lesson for himself (7:1–27). Or he can ponder the lazy man's
dilapidated property while walking by and take the matter to heart
(24:30–34): "I saw and considered it; I looked and received instruction" (24:32). Other times, people gain wisdom by reflecting on
animal behavior. Ants work hard and store up food, even without
a leader to command them, while laziness brings poverty (6:7–11).
Thus, "Go to the ant, O sluggard; consider her ways, and be wise"
(6:6).[7] Proverbs also frequently points to the broader natural world
and makes all sorts of analogies to help readers understand how
the moral life works: "Can a man carry fire next to his chest and
his clothes not be burned? Or can one walk on hot coals and his
feet not be scorched? So is he who goes in to his neighbor's wife;
none who touches her will go unpunished" (6:27–29). "Pressing
milk produces curds, pressing the nose produces blood, and pressing anger produces strife" (30:33). Men's behavior is like that of
eagles, serpents, and ships (30:18–19) and kings' behavior like that
of lions, roosters, and goats (30:29–31). Foolish human conduct
resembles both "clouds and wind without rain" (25:14) and "a bad
tooth or a foot that slips" (25:19).

---

[7] Earlier, I suggested that appealing to hibernating bears as a moral
example for humans is an illegitimate kind of "natural law" argument.
Readers may ask why it's legitimate to observe industrious ants and imitate
them but illegitimate to observe hibernating bears and imitate them. The
difference is that Proverbs 6 doesn't say: ants are industrious and therefore
humans should be industrious. Rather, Proverbs 6 assumes that we know
that having no food is a bad thing for us and thus that behavior tending
to make us poor is foolish and behavior tending to make us prosperous is
wise. We can look at ants and see a vivid example of how those who work
hard tend to have enough food, especially in contrast to what we so often
observe with lazy people. Thus, the appeal to ants is not so much to *prove*
that hard work is good but to *illustrate* what industriousness produces and
to *shame* lazy people.

None of these analogies or illustrations would make sense if the world were not filled with meaning, purpose, and order. Proverbs constantly assumes that there is a way the world is supposed to work and that we human beings can discern what that is. It is not that the world always works this way, but Proverbs expects us to recognize that something is off-kilter when it does not. Occasionally it snows in summer, just as sometimes a fool receives honor (26:1), but these instances stand outside the regular order of things, and wise people recognize that they are bizarre and unbecoming. This raises interesting questions about how exactly people should draw conclusions from observing the natural order. Chapter 6 will revisit Proverbs when focusing on such questions. But for now we can simply note again that the world has not slipped into meaningless chaos nor have sinful people lost all ability to learn about the moral life through reflecting upon it.

Nevertheless, readers may have one additional question that does require an answer here: Is it somewhat misleading to describe the people who gain wisdom in Proverbs as *sinners*? Proverbs was written for the old-covenant people of Israel, who had received God's saving grace. Was it only because they were *redeemed* that they could learn about the moral life through observing the natural order? Does Proverbs give us any confidence to conclude that *unbelieving* sinners can do the same?

Although Proverbs was written for God's covenant people, it also teaches that the pursuit of wisdom is not for redeemed people exclusively. For instance, near the beginning of wisdom's speech in Proverbs 8, she states that kings, rulers, princes, and nobles rule through her (8:15–16). But this does not refer only to Israelite authorities but to "all who govern justly" (8:16). Wherever we see justice done in the world, wisdom stands behind it. The presence of wisdom among Gentiles is also evident in several sections of Proverbs that were probably either adapted from non-Israelite sources or written by non-Israelites (22:17–24:22; 30:1–14; 31:1–9).[8] Other Old Testament texts also ascribe wisdom to Gentiles (e.g., 1 Kgs 4:30; Jer 49:7; Obad 8). Believers in the true God certainly have advantages over unbelievers in understanding the natural moral order, and chapter 5 will consider the importance of natural law for the *Christian* life specifically. But acquiring wisdom in the way Proverbs primarily describes it is not unique to people of faith.

Cosmic Nonsense

This chapter concludes by noting a few texts from the Old Testament prophets that further confirm the world's enduring meaning, purpose, and order and the implications for human morality. I borrow the term "cosmic nonsense" from John Barton, who has written helpfully about these texts in connection with natural law.[9] The basic idea in these texts is that there is a proper way that things work and that deviations from this order are bizarre and nonsensical. This is true for both the natural world and the moral life, and understanding the one helps us understand the other.

Amos provides a couple of examples. One of them asks rhetorically: "Do horses run on rocks? Does one plow there with oxen? But you have turned justice into poison and the fruit of righteousness into wormwood" (6:12). Rocks, horses, and oxen have certain characteristics, and however much one may want them to be otherwise, it is simply not so. Horses were made to run, and oxen were born to plow, but trying to make them do so on rocky ground is

---

[8] See DCMO, 393–95.

[9] See John Barton, *Understanding Old Testament Ethics: Approaches and Explorations* (Louisville: Westminster John Knox, 2003), 32–39.

stupid. It makes no sense and will not turn out well. Amos suggests that there is something similar about twisting justice and righteousness into something harmful and bitter. It is possible to do such things, of course, but it overturns the order of reality. Sin is not just wrong; it is bizarre.[10]

We see such notions in Isaiah especially. Isaiah seemed to envision a holistic order of reality in which each part has its proper place, including human beings. To resist this order is ludicrous, a moronic rebellion against the God who established it. At the opening of Isaiah, God lamented: "The ox knows its owner, and the donkey its master's crib, but Israel does not know, my people do not understand" (1:3). Even farm animals not known for their intelligence can understand the order of things. Rebelling against reality is, quite literally, worse than asinine. For humans to rebel against God turns reality on its head. Or consider Isa 5:20: "Woe to those who call evil good and good evil, who put darkness for light and light for darkness, who put bitter for sweet and sweet for bitter!" It is one thing to confuse items that are similar but quite another to confuse items that are completely opposite. Confusing opposites exposes a person's ignorance. Good and evil are diametrically different, and thus to call one the other is pure stupidity. Or, as Isaiah says later: "Shall the axe boast over him who hews with it, or the saw magnify itself against him who wields it? As if a rod should wield him who lifts it, or as if a staff should lift him who is not wood!" (10:15). This makes us laugh because it sounds like what we might see in a cartoon. Yet this is what human rulers are like who think they themselves, not God, are sovereign (10:5–14).

---

[10] See also Amos 3:3–6, which points to an established order that encompasses inanimate objects, animals, human beings, and even God himself.

Perhaps Isaiah's most powerful imagery along these lines comes in 29:15–16: "Ah, you who hide deep from the LORD your counsel, whose deeds are in the dark, and who say, 'Who sees us? Who knows us?' You turn things upside down! Shall the potter be regarded as the clay, that the thing made should say of its maker, 'He did not make me'; or the thing formed say of him who formed it, 'He has no understanding'?" Like Amos, Isaiah emphasizes not simply how wrong sin is but also how utterly bizarre it is. Clay lording it over the potter is the stuff of fantasy, of an alternative universe. Rebelling against God makes just as much sense. It is not just despicable; it is laughable.

None of these texts would work if the natural world is fundamentally chaotic and disordered. Bad things happen and strange things happen, but they are only *bad* and *strange* because there is a good and comprehensible order that God continues to uphold. To deviate from it cuts against the grain of the universe.[11]

---

[11] I use a phrase from the title of Stanley Hauerwas's Gifford Lectures, although I don't mean to suggest that I follow Hauerwas's conclusions. See *With the Grain of the Universe: The Church's Witness and Natural Theology* (Grand Rapids: Brazos, 2001).

3

Natural Law and Civil Justice

The first two chapters have argued that God reveals his moral will in the natural order. Although this natural order is fallen and under a divine curse, it remains meaningful and purposeful. God preserves it through the enduring Noahic covenant. As divine image-bearers, human beings are capable of understanding the natural order and the way of life fitting for creatures like themselves who live within it, yet they are deeply sinful and thus prone to misinterpret the world and rebel against its moral order.

If these things are true, what would we expect human societies to look like? We would anticipate seeing many horrors and tragedies as the diabolical effects of sin spread their roots. But there should also be evidence of the continuing testimony of natural law. We should see people getting married and having children. We should see people working and developing useful products. We should also see remnants of justice in human relationships. In short, we would expect things to be bad, but not nearly as bad as they might be. Amid much pain and loss, human life should also display much that is noble, just, and beautiful.

I imagine that most readers will agree that this matches their own experience of the world. This chapter inquires whether our experience matches Scripture's description of human life. To pursue this inquiry well, we need to be thoughtful about where we look for evidence. The Bible's main storyline concerns the history of God's unique covenant people: the family of Abraham, the nation of Israel, and the early new-covenant church.[1] Scripture is not a world history but a sacred history. Its story line focuses not on the covenant people's response to God's common grace known through natural revelation but on their response to God's gracious redemption known through special revelation. The effects of natural law in human societies are not Scripture's main interest.

Nevertheless, the Bible provides many glimpses of the world at large. God's covenant people have never lived in isolation from other human communities. As Scripture describes his people's interaction with these other communities, we pick up indirect insight about the work of natural law in pagan human societies. This chapter explores evidence that unbelieving individuals and societies have knowledge and appreciation of what is just. This sort of knowledge and understanding is difficult or impossible to explain without the reality of natural law. I find this evidence first in the fascinating

---

[1] I hold to a classical Reformed view of the biblical covenants, as summarized in the Westminster Confession of Faith, chap. 7. That is, there's one people of God through redemptive history, and the Abrahamic, Mosaic, and new covenants are administrations of an organically unified "covenant of grace." I put things in ways that reflect that view, but I don't think my main claims about natural law are dependent upon it.

encounter between Abraham and Abimelech in Genesis 20. After
a brief study of the natural law concepts present in Genesis 20, we
will then consider how these ideas show up in subsequent biblical
stories and reinforce the conclusions suggested by that earlier text.
The chapter concludes by reflecting on additional evidence from
Mosaic law and the New Testament.

Abraham and Abimelech

For most Christians, Genesis 20 is not one of the more memorable
biblical stories. But for those interested in natural law or in political life, it is a fascinating and thought-provoking account. Here we
watch a confrontation between two very different parties. In one
corner stands Abraham, the man of faith to whom God made great
covenant promises (Genesis 12, 15, and 17). In the other corner
is Abimelech, a Gentile king of the city of Gerar. He lived outside God's covenant with Abraham and was ignorant of its saving
promises. How would the pagan Abimelech treat Abraham when
he journeyed into his territory? How would Abimelech respond
when a conflict arose between them? What happened in their
interaction is perhaps not what we would have anticipated, especially considering that this story immediately follows the account
of the vile Gentile city of Sodom (Genesis 18–19). Perhaps the
story of Sodom tempts us to conclude that no testimony of natural
law remains in this fallen world. But if so, Genesis 20 corrects us.
Natural law continues to press its claims, and some individuals and
societies outside of God's covenant people are paying attention.[2]

---

[2] For an interesting discussion of this text, similar to mine in several
respects, see also David Novak, *The Jewish Social Contract: An Essay in
Political Theology* (Princeton, NJ: Princeton University Press, 2005), 40–46.

Such stories have special relevance for Christian readers thinking about natural law. Genesis frequently describes Abraham as *sojourning*, for he did not have a permanent home. He lived in tents and journeyed among other people's cities. The New Testament tells new-covenant Christians that they, too, are sojourners (1 Pet 2:11), alerting us to the fact that our lives in this world have fundamental similarities to Abraham's. Of course, many Christians own homes or have some other permanent dwelling. But Christians are nevertheless sojourners because we are away from our true home. Christ's heavenly, new-creation kingdom is the place of our citizenship (Phil 3:20), our lasting city (Heb 13:12), and our very life (Col 3:1–3). The Jerusalem above is our mother (Gal 4:26). Thus, as long as we remain in this present world, Christians are sojourners, away from where we really belong. The point is that Christians around the world live among different kinds of people and in different kinds of societies. Some of these people are like Abimelech, and some of these societies are like Gerar. We need to have a conception of natural law to be able to explain this.

The Conflict

Abraham was on the move again in Genesis 20, and he "sojourned in Gerar" (v. 1). Readers know nothing about Gerar at this point. Apparently, Abraham did not know much about it either, for he made a major misjudgment. The text tells us that he "said of Sarah his wife, 'She is my sister'" (20:2). Abraham had tried this before, in Egypt, because he feared they would take Sarah and also kill him if they thought he was her husband (12:11–13). We assume he acted for similar reasons here in Gerar. He must have thought Gerar was a dangerous place, where the inhabitants kill men to take their wives. The story later confirms that Abraham thought the worst about this city: "I did it because I thought, 'There is no fear of God at all in this place, and they will kill me because of my wife'" (20:11).

Abraham's concerns were not entirely misplaced, for King Abimelech "sent and took Sarah" (20:2). But God said to Abimelech in a dream: "Behold, you are a dead man because of the woman whom you have taken, for she is a man's wife" (20:3). Abimelech proceeded to protest his people's innocence since Abraham and Sarah had told him she was his sister (20:5). God agreed that Abimelech had taken Sarah "in the integrity of [his] heart" and for that reason had not allowed Abimelech to touch her. He told Abimelech to return Sarah or else face death (20:6–7).

A few initial observations: God's nocturnal conversation with Abimelech is mysterious. Readers have no idea whether God had spoken to Abimelech before. But there is no evidence of any intimate or redemptive relationship between the two of them. God spoke merely as Governor of the world and Judge of human affairs, in a way that reflects his relationship to the world under the Noahic covenant. So, it seems proper to regard Abimelech as an unbeliever and to refer to him as a pagan in the traditional sense of one who worshiped false gods. Furthermore, the moral problem at issue in this story involves taking a *married* woman. This is the crux of God's accusation and Abimelech's claim of innocence. It is difficult not to feel alarmed by the mere fact that Abimelech "took" Sarah, no matter who she was, and this is a reminder that Gerar was far from idyllic. But the writer wanted to emphasize that even if Gerar's king took women for his harem, he did not take *married* women, and this is not a small detail. Finally, it is important to note for the discussion that follows that God did not inform Abimelech that adultery is wrong and deserves judgment. Abimelech already knew that. God simply informed Abimelech that he had unwittingly taken someone's wife. So, Abimelech rose early, assembled his servants, and reported what he had learned. "And the men were very much afraid" (20:8). Abimelech then summoned Abraham and confronted him about what he had done (20:9).

These verses communicate alarm and earnestness among Abimelech and his servants. Abimelech got up *early*. His men were *very afraid*. It is difficult to tell whether they were genuinely conscience-stricken or simply terrified that God would destroy them as he had destroyed Sodom. But in either case Abimelech's men took this morally problematic situation seriously. We should also notice that Abimelech initiated judicial proceedings against Abraham.[3] He did not gather his army and punish him without trial. As we will see in the following verses, he was angry with Abraham but would give him an opportunity to defend himself.

The Resolution

We have already seen considerable evidence that Gerar was not nearly as bad as Abraham suspected. The trial scene not only confirms this but also explains why this city respected the claims of justice to the degree it did: (1) the people of Gerar recognized certain moral boundaries in human relations that should not be breeched, and (2) they acknowledged their accountability to an authority higher than themselves. The natural law lurks behind both of these.

The first evidence—respect of moral boundaries—appears in Abimelech's opening words to Abraham: "What have you done to

---

[3] On the judicial nature of their encounter, see e.g., James K. Bruckner, *Implied Law in the Abraham Narrative: A Literary and Theological Analysis* (Sheffield, UK: Sheffield Academic, 2001), 173; and Terrence E. Fretheim, *The Book of Genesis* (Nashville: Abingdon, 1994), 482.

us? And how have I sinned against you, that you have brought on me and my kingdom a great sin? You have done to me things that ought not to be done" (20:9). This last line is particularly interesting. Abimelech and Abraham were strangers to each other in basically every respect. One was a king living in a city, the other a nomad living in tents. Abimelech was from a town near the Mediterranean, while Abraham had spent most of his life in the faraway lands of Ur and Haran (11:27–31). They practiced different religions, belonged to different peoples, and thus followed different customs. But despite being cultural strangers to one another, Abimelech saw moral commonality between them. There were "things that ought not to be done"—things that humans simply should not do to one another, no matter where they are from, what people group they belong to, or their stations in life. Taking another man's wife or passing off one's wife as his sister belongs in this category. Abimelech knew this and knew that Abraham knew it, which is why Abimelech was so outraged by the latter's actions.

The second detail that explains the presence of justice in Gerar—acknowledging a higher authority to which all are accountable—appears in the next verses: "And Abimelech said to Abraham, 'What did you see, that you did this thing?' Abraham said, 'I did it because I thought, 'There is no fear of God at all in this place, and they will kill me because of my wife'" (20:10–11). When we read this, we can only conclude that *Abraham badly misjudged the moral character of this city*. The reason he acted as he did is because he thought Gerar lacked the fear of God, but events proved otherwise. Abimelech and his officials feared God in the literal sense that when God threatened to destroy them, they returned Sarah to Abraham immediately. But Abraham did not know God would speak directly to Gerar's king, so he must have meant something different by "the fear of God." Abraham seemed to refer to some general respect for divine authority that restrains people from doing egregious things—things that ought not to be done. Abraham thought Gerar lacked this fear of God, but Gerar did not.

Genesis 20 provides compelling evidence of natural law. Where would Abimelech have gained this knowledge of trans-cultural moral boundaries? Why would he be justified in expecting Abraham to abide by these boundaries within Gerar when he had never been there? From where would he have learned the fear of God even before God spoke to him in a dream? There must have been some universally accessible source of knowledge of God and his basic moral requirements. Unless we assume (without any biblical evidence) that God had been delivering special revelation to all human societies of Abraham's day, the only plausible conclusion is that God had maintained the testimony of natural law and that it was restraining some pagan peoples from bad behavior.

The Fear of God and Things That Ought Not to Be Done

Several subsequent biblical texts refer to the fear of God and things that ought not to be done. These texts confirm the conclusions just drawn from Genesis 20. Thus, we find further evidence of the reality of natural law and its beneficial effects even in pagan societies—as well as of the terrible consequences when people despise the fear of God and pursue what should never be done.

Things That Ought Not to Be Done

Two other texts in Genesis refer to things that ought not to be done. As in Genesis 20, both stories involve conflicts between moral strangers: those belonging to the covenant line of Abraham and those outside this line. The circumstances of each story differ from those of Genesis 20 in important ways, yet even these differences in detail showcase the importance of natural law.

One text is Genesis 34. This tells a story about the family of Jacob, grandson of Abraham, after he had returned to Canaan after living many years with his uncle Laban in Paddan-aram. Jacob's daughter Dinah had gone out to socialize with the Gentile women of the land (34:1). While doing so, she caught the attention of Shechem, son of Hamor the local king. Shechem "seized her and lay with her and humiliated her" (34:2). Shechem then asked his father to get her for him as a wife (34:3–4). Hamor thus initiated a conversation with Jacob, who apparently responded with restraint (3:5–6). But when Dinah's brothers heard the news and came in from the field, they "were indignant and very angry." Shechem had done "an outrageous thing," and "such a thing must not be done" (34:7). The rest of the chapter narrates how the brothers pretended to make a deal with Hamor to give Dinah in marriage and then, against their father's pragmatic wishes, slaughtered all the men of the city.

Like Genesis 20, Genesis 34 describes a conflict between the covenant household and a pagan city, and it, too, concerns sex and marriage. But this conflict is the mirror image of the earlier one. Instead of Abraham transgressing a universal moral boundary and wronging a pagan city, here the rulers of a pagan city transgress a universal moral boundary and wrong Abraham's descendants. Abimelech exhibited fear of God when he refused to seize the wives of those sojourning in his territory and took Sarah as an apparently unmarried older woman, likely with Abraham's (grudging?) consent. But Shechem grabbed a young girl and raped her without her family's knowledge. Jacob's sons appealed not to a special law God had given them but to universal moral norms. A prince who

violated a young girl who entered his city to socialize did something
no one should ever do. It is precisely the sort of behavior that pro-
voked God to send the great flood (6:2).[4] We can see, therefore, that
moral expectations work in both directions, as we would expect if
natural law remains a potent force in the world. Guests who enter
a foreign city ought to observe universal moral boundaries (which
Abraham failed to do in Genesis 20), and rulers ought to observe
universal moral boundaries toward guests in their city (as Shechem
failed to do in Genesis 34). Some believers and unbelievers alike
observe these boundaries, and some believers and unbelievers alike
transgress them. But all victims are rightly outraged.

The other text that refers to things not to be done is Genesis 29, which narrates an earlier event in Jacob's life. Jacob had fled
from his brother, Esau, to the home of his uncle Laban in Paddan-
aram (Genesis 28). There he fell in love with his cousin Rachel and
agreed to work for Laban for seven years in exchange for her hand
in marriage. At the end of these years, Laban threw a marriage cere-
mony but secretly substituted his older and less attractive daughter,
Leah. Jacob spent the night with Leah and discovered what happened only the next morning (29:1–25). Jacob confronted Laban
the way Abimelech confronted Abraham: "What is this you have
done to me?" (29:25). Laban defended himself by saying: "It is not
so done in our country, to give the younger before the firstborn"
but agreed to give him Rachel in exchange for seven more years of
work (29:26–27). In the original Hebrew text, what is translated

---

[4] For arguments that Gen 6:2 refers to kings taking women for their
harems, see, e.g., David Novak, *Natural Law in Judaism* (Cambridge:
Cambridge University Press, 1997), 36–37; and Rita F. Cefalu, "Royal
Priestly Heirs to the Restoration Promise of Genesis 3:15: A Biblical
Theological Perspective on the Sons of God in Genesis 6," *Westminster
Theological Journal* 76 (2014): 356–67.

here as "it is not so done" is similar to the "ought not to be done" statements in the two other texts we have examined.

Readers of the earlier Jacob stories do not feel sorry for him at this point. After all, Jacob had deceived his father, Isaac, to get his older brother's blessing (Genesis 27), so it was poetic justice when Laban deceived him. Jacob got what he deserved. Still, we do not find Laban's self-defense persuasive. Reading Genesis 20 and 34, we think it obvious that Abraham's deceit and Shechem's rape violated universal moral boundaries, but the need to marry off one's older daughter before a younger one does not seem obvious at all. The text itself supports these intuitions. Careful readers may have noted that Laban's statement had an important difference from those of Abimelech and Dinah's brothers: Laban said that this is a thing not to be done "*in our country.*" Marrying older daughters first was a local custom, not a universal moral boundary understood through natural law. No one can rightly expect a visitor in a foreign country to have knowledge of this custom. This explains why we judge Laban to be a scoundrel.

The Fear of God

Genesis 20:11 implies that the people of Gerar had a fear of God that restrained them from at least some evil conduct. Since Scripture often describes godly believers as having "the fear of the Lord," it may be puzzling to find this text ascribing "the fear of God" to a Gentile pagan. But this reference is not an anomaly, for several other texts in Genesis, Exodus, and Deuteronomy also mention the fear of God with respect to Gentiles. This fear of God is obviously important for understanding life in the world.

Two of these texts communicate that the fear of God sometimes constrains those with civil authority (as with Abimelech in

Genesis 20).[5] The first, Genesis 42, narrates the journey of Jacob's
sons to Egypt to buy grain during a famine. The sons were unaware
that their brother Joseph, whom they had sold into slavery years
before, was now second-in-command to Pharaoh. Joseph recognized them, but they did not recognize him. Joseph accused them
of coming to spy on the land and put them in jail for three days
(42:1–17). At this point, Joseph provided a way to prove their
innocence. He introduced his offer in this way: "Do this and you
will live, for I fear God" (42:18). Joseph's point was that he would
treat them justly. He would not keep them imprisoned without
trying to resolve the facts in dispute. This is because he had the
fear of God.

Of course, Joseph belonged to the house of Abraham, so one
might object that this text is not a good example of the fear of
God among pagan Gentiles. But remember that Joseph was hid-
ing his identity from his brothers. They thought he was a pagan
Gentile, and he wanted them to keep thinking this for a while.
So, how could Joseph communicate to them that he, a pagan
Gentile ruler, would treat them justly? He appealed to his fear
of God. This was evidently something that both a prince in
Pharaoh's house and the covenant people, nomads from Canaan,
could understand.

The other example of the fear of God restraining civil officials takes us to the story of Israel traveling through the wilderness
after leaving Egypt. Before they reached Sinai and received the law,
Moses's father-in-law Jethro (or Reuel) paid him a visit. Jethro was
certainly a Gentile (Exod 2:15–16; 18:1), but it is not immediately

---

[5] For an example in the other direction, consider the unjust judge
of Jesus's parable in Luke 18:4, who describes himself as one who doesn't
fear God.

clear whether we should consider him a pagan. Exodus 2:16 calls him a "priest" but does not tell us what sort of priest. When Jethro visited Moses in the wilderness, he rejoiced in the good things the Lord had done for Israel and blessed the Lord (18:9–10). This may argue against calling him a pagan. Nevertheless, Jethro then said: "Now I know that the LORD is greater than all gods, because in this affair they [the Egyptians] dealt arrogantly with the people" (18:11). This indicates that Jethro at least *was* a pagan until just then. He may have heard of the LORD, but he regarded him as simply one god among many. Whether or not Jethro's subsequent sacrifice and fellowship with Aaron and the Israelite elders (18:12) indicate his conversion to worshiping the true God alone, Jethro's pagan background is important to keep in mind when reading the rest of Exodus 18.

The day after his arrival, Jethro watched Moses judge the people from morning till evening (18:13). Although his son-in-law was eighty years old (Exod 7:7), Jethro did what fathers-in-law often do: he gave Moses unsolicited advice. His proposal, which Moses accepted (18:24–26) and later incorporated into the Mosaic law (Deut 1:9–18), called for delegating most of the work to other leaders and reserving the difficult cases for himself (Exod 18:14–23). Jethro suggested the following credentials for the judges: "Look for able men from all the people, men who fear God, who are trustworthy and hate a bribe" (18:21). If Jethro was not a pagan, that had only been true for a day, so realistically we expect him to evaluate Israel's judicial procedures in a way that reflects his past (pagan) experience. His proposal reflects little more than common sense, in no way depending on Israel's special relationship with the Lord. As he spoke from this perspective, Jethro appealed to the fear of God as a key characteristic of a just judge. To fear God, in his mind, goes hand in hand with being trustworthy and refusing bribes.

Once again, the fear of God is something both pagan and covenant believer can understand.[6]

Another important example of the fear of God among pagan Gentiles comes in the fascinating account of the midwives in Exodus 1. Here we see the fear of God inspiring ordinary people to defy the injustice of the powerful. Pharaoh, trying to suppress the perceived threat from his Hebrew slaves, ordered two midwives to kill all the Hebrew baby boys at birth. The text first calls these women "Hebrew midwives" (1:15), which may give the impression that they themselves were Hebrews. But the text immediately clarifies in what sense they were "Hebrew" midwives: they served "the Hebrew women" (1:16). These women were Egyptian. Pharaoh would surely not have entrusted the slaughter of Hebrew babies to Hebrew women, nor would he have found the midwives' insult of Hebrew women (1:19) convincing coming from Hebrew women themselves.[7]

Although they were Egyptian, and thus surely pagans, the midwives "feared God and did not do as the king of Egypt commanded them, but let the male children live" (1:17). A few verses later the text again says that they feared God (1:21). Pharaoh decreed genocide. He obviously did not fear God. But divine fear inspired at least two of Pharaoh's subjects to defy his order and to

---

[6] There are other possible examples of pagan rulers instructing Israel's leaders in the fear of God (without using that phrase). For example, in 2 Chr 36:13, King Nebuchadnezzar of Babylon required King Zedekiah of Judah to call God as witness through an oath, yet the Israelite king broke that oath. Also, in a letter King Artaxerxes of Persia gave to Ezra when sending him to Jerusalem, Artaxerxes expressed concern that his decrees for God's house be carried out, lest God's "wrath be against the realm of the king and his sons" (Ezra 7:23).

[7] See Novak, *Natural Law in Judaism*, 49–50.

persist in it even when he confronted them personally (1:18–19). So, we see that the presence or absence of the fear of God in both rulers and subjects can make an enormous difference in whether justice is done.

The final example is a negative one, but it confirms this conclusion. Amid many chapters laying out various laws for Israel, Deut 25:17 pauses to urge the Israelites, "Remember what Amalek did to you on the way as you came out of Egypt" (see Exod 17:8–16). Amalek did not simply wage war. "He attacked you on the way when you were faint and weary, and cut off your tail, those who were lagging behind you," Moses recalled (Deut 25:18). In contemporary parlance, the Amalekites were war criminals who intentionally targeted vulnerable civilians. The text then adds a brief conclusion: Amalek "did not fear God" (25:18). The implications are clear: Israel must remember the Amalekites because what they did was an unusually terrible atrocity. Most Gentile pagans do not behave in so brutal a way. If the reason Amalek did what it did is because it lacked the fear of God, the reason other pagan peoples do not act this way is because some fear of God remains among them.

We should not confuse the "fear of God" in these texts with the fear of the Lord that is a mark of true godliness. But the presence or absence of the fear of God evidently makes a big difference for the well-being of human societies. The fear of God is what distinguishes unbelievers who are war criminals from those who respect marriage and judicial procedure. It emboldens ordinary unbelievers to defy tyrannical rulers. Where do such God-fearers get their rudimentary knowledge of God and his moral will since they do not get it from special revelation and a redemptive covenant relationship? It must come from natural revelation. Sinners so often resist the testimony of natural law, to be sure, but it continues to make its presence felt.

Natural Law and Pagan Society in Other Biblical Texts

The opening books of Scripture narrate the fall into sin and describe many of its terrible consequences. But through ideas such as "the fear of God" and "things that ought not to be done," these books also make clear that unredeemed sinners retain substantial moral knowledge and that some of them follow its instruction to a remarkable extent, to the great benefit of human society. The discussion of these themes has thus confirmed the conclusions of the first two chapters. In this final section of chapter 3, we will examine additional biblical evidence that provides similar confirmation. I turn first to the Mosaic law and then conclude with some brief comments from the New Testament.

Mosaic Law and Ancient Near Eastern Law

Various features of the Mosaic law provide interesting evidence of the reality and importance of the natural law.[8] This section examines just one line of evidence, the similarities between the Mosaic law and other legal documents of Israel's neighbors in the ancient Near East. The basic point is this: if the divinely inspired Mosaic law could borrow as much as it did from ancient Near Eastern law, the legal systems of Israel's pagan neighbors must have captured much that is just, and only the work of natural law can explain this.

For the most part, Scripture uses literary forms already present in the cultures in which those forms arose. The Psalms were not the first poems in history, nor were Paul's epistles the first letters. The same is true for the Mosaic law. Human societies produced

---

[8] For lengthy discussion, see DCMO, chap. 7.

legal codes long before Israel left Egypt, and many such documents from the ancient Near East are known to us today. The Mosaic law is like these documents in many respects. Moses and whoever else contributed to writing the law must have been familiar with them. We will see this by focusing on the so-called Covenant Code of Exod 20:23–23:19.

One similarity is the use of *case law*. Rather than give long lists of detailed rules, the Covenant Code mostly presents a small number of concrete cases: when a man strikes his slave (Exod 21:20), when a man strikes a pregnant woman (21:22), when an ox gores a man (21:28), if a fire breaks out (22:6), and so on. Modern legal codes often strive to be comprehensive. They try to anticipate all sorts of scenarios and leave as little room for judges' discretion as possible. In contrast, ancient Near Eastern codes sought to illustrate the way disputes should be decided, leaving much to the wisdom of judges to resolve new cases in ways resembling the resolution of the example cases.[9] It is debatable whether this is the best way to construct a legal code. But the case-law approach of the ancient Near East must have provided at least a modestly effective way to secure justice, or else God's law for Israel would surely not have used it.

It is also interesting to note, second, that the Covenant Code often used the same cases found in other ancient Near Eastern codes. The case of fire breaking out in a field is one example.[10] Even some odd cases that could not have been common, such as what to do when an ox gores a person to death, appear in multiple legal

---

[9] Cf. Jonathan Burnside, *God, Justice, and Society: Aspects of Law and Legality in the Bible* (Oxford: Oxford University Press, 2011), 5.

[10] See Exod 22:6; and the Laws of Hammurabi (LH) 105–6. For translation of the latter, see *Ancient Codes and Laws of the Near East*, vol. 2, *The Babylonian Laws*, ed. G. R. Driver and John C. Miles (Oxford, UK: Clarendon, 1955).

documents.[11] The Covenant Code's use of such cases must have been intentional, not coincidental. This suggests that such cases, however odd they may appear, must have served as *good* illustrations of how to resolve analogous kinds of controversies.

Third, the Covenant Code and other ancient Near Eastern legal texts recognize many of the same civil law categories. The Code of Hammurabi, for example, examines disputes concerning disrespect for authority, murder, adultery, theft, and lying. It treats these actions as wrong and prescribes punishments and remedies for them. The Mosaic law addresses similar issues.

Finally, the Covenant Code uses some of the same sorts of punishments and remedies as the ancient Near Eastern documents. The *lex talionis* is a prominent example. This "law of retaliation" requires "eye for an eye" and "tooth for a tooth." The first provision of the Code of Hammurabi (and many subsequent provisions) prescribes the *lex talionis*. It also appears in the Covenant Code and elsewhere in the Mosaic law.[12] This must have been an effective principle of justice. It may not appear that way initially, but when we remember that the *lex talionis* often was not applied literally but served as a principle of justice—the punishment ought to fit the crime—we can appreciate why the Mosaic law was happy to borrow it from surrounding cultures.[13]

These considerations point us to an inevitable conclusion: the legal systems of the ancient Near East must have captured much that is just. To be sure, the Mosaic law also changed many things in these documents, which is exactly what we would expect as it

---

[11] Exod 21:28–32; and LH 250–52.

[12] LH 1; and Exod 21:23–25; cf. Lev 24:19–20; Deut 19:21.

[13] See PAC, 259–66. Cf. William Ian Miller, *Eye for an Eye* (Cambridge: Cambridge University Press, 2006).

borrowed material from pagan cultures and applied it to God's holy people.[14] The ancient Near East was a sinful place. It had no special divine revelation or redemptive relationship with God. But it was evidently not devoid of justice, thus giving further witness to the ongoing influence of the natural law.

Natural Law in Pagan Communities: The New Testament

The New Testament offers no single example as striking as what we just observed with the Mosaic law. But several smaller examples reinforce this chapter's conclusions thus far. The early Christians proclaimed the gospel in Mediterranean cultures ruled by the pagan and deeply sinful Roman Empire. Yet even in this context we see the New Testament recognize genuine goodness and justice among the peoples it called out of darkness into the light.

We see this first in what the New Testament says about civil government. Several texts call Christians to honor and submit to their political officials, whom God appointed as his own servants to punish evildoers, for Christians' benefit (e.g., Rom 13:1–7; 1 Pet 2:13–17). These texts raise many practical questions about how far to obey and when to resist. Nevertheless, it is difficult to see how civil authorities could be *God's* servants, who carry out *his* vengeance and wrath, for Christians' own good, if they did not promote and preserve at least many good things in society. Roman law and Roman magistrates evidently had insight into what is morally good, and they must have attained this through natural revelation. The presence of justice in the Roman legal system is also evident in Acts. Paul encountered a number of Roman officials in this book.

---

[14] See DCMO, 294–98.

He consistently showed them honor and deference, even when they failed him. But many of them actually made fairly sensible judgments and acknowledged limits to their authority (e.g., Acts 16:38–39; 18:14–16; 19:35–41; 22:25–29; 23:16–35; 27:42–43). Even a perceived troublemaker such as Paul could often find justice in Roman courts.

Second, Paul's so-called household codes in Eph 5:22–6:9 and Col 3:18–4:1 suggest that the Greco-Roman world must have understood some important things about family life correctly. The codes, both in form and content, bear many similarities to common ethical teaching in the broader culture.[15] It is difficult to imagine how Paul, as divinely inspired, could have borrowed this material if it did not reflect much that was good, despite so much sexual immorality in the Greco-Roman world.

Finally, the fact that the New Testament sometimes respects and even relies upon the moral judgment of non-Christians is striking, given the emphasis elsewhere on *not* thinking the way pagans do (e.g., Rom 12:2; 2 Cor 10:4–5). Paul urges readers to walk "properly" (1 Thess 4:12) and "in wisdom" before "outsiders" (Col 4:5), indicating that non-Christians have enough moral sense to be repelled from Christianity by believers who act badly. Paul also requires that church officers "be well thought of by outsiders" (1 Tim 3:7). The New Testament recognizes, of course, that wicked people sometimes despise Christians for holy behavior (e.g., 1 Pet 4:4). But Paul must have thought that pagans generally

---

[15] See for example Andrew T. Lincoln, "Excursus: 'The Household Code': Its Origin and Adaptation," in *The New Interpreter's Bible*, vol. 11 (Nashville: Abingdon, 2000), 652–54; and Markus Bockmuehl, *Jewish Law in Gentile Churches: Halakha and the Beginning of Christian Public Ethics* (Grand Rapids: Baker Academic, 2000), 128.

have enough moral acuity to recognize when a person is hypocritical or foolish. When pagans accurately draw such a conclusion about someone who professes Christ, it should alert the church that this person is unfit for ecclesiastical office. Finally, several of Paul's exhortations in Titus 2 assume some good moral judgment among unbelievers. Older women's good conduct would keep the word of God from being "reviled" (2:5), younger men's holiness would keep opponents from having anything "evil to say about us" (2:8), and slaves' godliness would "adorn the doctrine of God our Savior" (2:10). The New Testament acknowledges that sometimes unbelievers slander Christians unjustly (e.g., 1 Pet 4:14–16). But if Christians act decently, Titus 2 presumes that unbelievers will generally lose their zeal for slandering them and instead recognize that the gospel of Christ produces good fruit in its adherents.[16]

Conclusion

At the outset of the chapter, I suggested that if God has indeed maintained the purpose and order of the world and still reveals his natural law, we would expect to see evidence of this in human societies, even among pagans. We have now observed such evidence in Scripture. The natural law continues to bear witness in this world, and that witness is not without effect.

This biblical material should provide modest encouragement for Christians today. Christians' hope for decisive relief from evil should be nothing short of Christ's second coming (e.g., 2 Thess 1:5–10). But until then we live in societies that are fundamentally

---

[16] See also 1 Cor 5:1, where Paul shames the Corinthian church for putting up with a sexual sin in their midst that "is not tolerated even among pagans."

similar to those that hosted Abraham and his family. For all the obvious cultural and technological differences, those societies and ours are filled with unbelievers with whom God's sojourning covenant people must try to live in peace (e.g., Rom 12:18). Unbelievers will often do terrible things, and Christians will suffer. But as with Abraham, sinful corruption is not the only thing Christians see in their societies. Our courts often do what is just, and non-Christians make sacrifices to promote the good. Abraham and his family were able to enter covenantal partnerships with relatively just kings such as Abimelech (Gen 21:22–34; 26:26–31). So also, Christians today may seek fruitful cooperation with at least some non-Christians for advancing what is good and just in the civil societies we share.

4

Natural Law, God's Universal Judgment, and the Gospel of Christ

In the previous chapter we were able to reflect on some relatively good news. Since God has preserved the purpose and order of the world, and thus maintains the testimony of his natural law to all people, there continues to be a measure of peace and justice in human societies. Things are far from perfect, but many people recognize that certain things "ought not to be done" and retain some fear of God. In many locales, Christians can pursue productive lives alongside unbelievers and have a reasonable prospect of receiving justice when wronged. We should be grateful to God for such things.

But Christians also know that these earthly blessings are only temporary. Scripture often calls the Lord a God of wrath and vengeance (e.g., Deut 32:35; Jer 51:56). In the Noahic covenant,

God promised to postpone the final judgment, but not to cancel it. This sobering reality prompts a question raised in the first chapter: On what basis does God hold all the world accountable to his judgment? A just God will surely not punish people for doing things they had no idea were wrong. Some people have heard or read God's will as revealed in the Scriptures, but what about the multitude that has not? The ongoing testimony of the natural law answers this question. Indeed, it provides the only possible answer, for without natural revelation the great multitude that lacks special revelation would receive no communication from God at all. Such people would have no relationship with God, and he could hardly accuse them of sinning against him.

Most of this chapter explores this theme. We will look first at some oracles of Old Testament prophets against Gentile nations. These nations had no knowledge of the Mosaic law, yet the prophets insisted they were responsible for their sins and that divine judgment was at hand. Natural law looms powerfully in the background. When we turn to Rom 1:18–2:16, where Paul sweeps all people under the righteous judgment of God, we find natural law in the foreground. Paul clarifies what the Old Testament oracles implied: God reveals his moral will to all people in what he has made and impresses his law upon their hearts. No one can plead excuse when called before his throne.

This is a sobering Christian doctrine, but we can be thankful that God's universal judgment is not the end of the story, nor is it even the last word when it comes to natural law. I began the chapter by referring to the *relatively* good news that God maintains the testimony of natural law. In contrast, the gospel of Christ is *absolutely* good news. It promises rescue from the final judgment, not merely postponement. Understood in these terms, the gospel makes no sense apart from divine judgment against sin.

There would be no need for the gospel if God's judgment did not stand against us. Thus, when the opening sections of this chapter explore the relationship of God's judgment and natural law, they simultaneously prepare the way for understanding the gospel. The final section of the chapter will make this explicit. We will reflect on how the reality of natural law ensures that the gospel message is understandable and relevant for all people to whom it is preached.

The Prophetic Oracles against Gentile Nations

The prophetical books take up a large share of the Old Testament.[1] The prophets wrote these books for Israel, and thus for the most part they address the Israelites directly. But many of these books also contain oracles against Gentile nations. Most likely, few if any of them were delivered to these foreign peoples, for the prophets wrote these oracles for the benefit of Israel—sometimes to warn Israel but also to provide comfort and encouragement. The oracles have various purposes. Some of them prophesy of a time when God will extend his salvation to these nations, pointing ahead to the ministry of the New Testament church. But more often the oracles pronounce judgment against these Gentiles for their wickedness.

The oracles of judgment are of special interest here. Gentile nations were not in a special covenantal relationship with God. They had not stood at Mount Sinai with Israel and received the

---

[1] The "prophetical books" refer to the final seventeen books of the Old Testament. Isaiah, Jeremiah, and Ezekiel are called the "major prophets" and the books of Hosea through Malachi the "minor prophets."

Torah. Yet God held them responsible for their sins. This places the issue of natural law squarely before us.[2]

What sorts of sins did these oracles address? At the final judgment, God will call people to account for *all* they have done (e.g., Matt 12:36; Heb 4:13), but these prophetic oracles only address certain kinds of shocking, notorious sins. The oracles focus on two kinds of (related) wrongs: first, the pride or *hubris* of these Gentile peoples and, second, the excessive, over-the-top injustices they perpetrate against others (against Israel especially but not exclusively). Why these two? The previous chapter points to an answer. Being inflated with hubris is the exact opposite of *the fear of God*. And those perpetrating over-the-top injustices do *things that ought not to be done*. The same basic criteria that Genesis and Exodus used for evaluating the moral character of Gentile people reappear here in the Old Testament prophets.

Another way to think about this is in terms of the Noahic covenant, by which God preserves and governs this fallen world. The prophetic oracles generally declare God's judgment *within* history, not the final judgment at the end of history. Thus, we would expect these oracles to judge the nations according to the standards of the Noahic covenant. But that covenant only focuses on basic things necessary for the survival of human societies, especially being fruitful, multiplying, and enforcing justice in the face of violence (Gen 9:1, 6–7). It does not mention the many smaller wrongs we do to each other every day, or even idolatry. God shows much long-suffering on these matters, for the time being. Keeping these observations in mind will help make sense of what the prophetic oracles denounce. They focus on those egregious things that threaten the

---

[2] For more detailed discussion of natural law in these prophetic oracles, see DCMO, 167–96.

existence of human societies at their core: an overweening hubris (lack of the fear of God) that tends to result in notorious acts of injustice (things that ought not to be done). We will now examine these themes in the oracles themselves.

Hubris

Perhaps the most striking feature about the oracles against Gentile nations is how often the prophets denounce them for overweening pride. This section provides brief examples from all three of the major prophets and one minor prophet. Many other texts could also illustrate the point (Isa 14:4, 11–15; 23:9; Jer 48:14, 42; 49:4, 16; 50:29–32; Ezek 30:6, 18; 31:10; 32:12; Hab 1:11; 2:4–5; Zech 9:6; 10:11).

Consider first a couple of texts from Isaiah. In an oracle against Babylon, God said he would "put an end to the pomp of the arrogant, and lay low the pompous pride of the ruthless" (Isa 13:11). Then "Babylon, the glory of kingdoms, the splendor and pomp of the Chaldeans, will be like Sodom and Gomorrah when God overthrew them" (13:19). In an oracle against Moab, Isaiah also notes, "We have heard of the pride of Moab—how proud he is!—of his arrogance, his pride, and his insolence; in his idle boasting he is not right" (16:6). Jeremiah says almost the same thing: "We have heard of the pride of Moab—he is very proud—of his loftiness, his pride, and his arrogance, and the haughtiness of his heart. I know his insolence, declares the LORD; his boasts are false, his deeds are false" (Jer 48:29–30). But not just Babylon and Moab—Ezekiel directs a similar charge against Tyre: "Your heart is proud, and you have said, 'I am a god. I sit in the seat of the gods, in the heart of the seas.' . . . You make your heart like the heart of a god" (Ezek 28:2). Zephaniah adds another voice accusing Moab, along with Ammon, of hubris: "This shall be their lot in return for their pride, because they taunted and boasted against the people of the LORD of hosts" (Zeph 2:10). Nineveh was little different: "This is the exultant city that lived securely, that said in her heart, 'I am, and there is no one else'" (2:15).

While all sin is against God and insults him, hubris defies God in an especially egregious way. A person who exalts himself as exceedingly wonderful is not just self-deluded but, in effect, dethrones the God who actually is supremely good, powerful, wise, and honorable. Hubris and the fear of God are diametrically opposed. This is explicit in some of the texts just quoted: Tyre's pride led her to say, "I am a god" (Ezek 28:2). Nineveh's boast—"I am, and there is no one else" (Zeph 2:15)—is what the true God says about himself (e.g., Isa 43:11). To think about this in connection with the previous chapter: these prophetic oracles condemn Gentile peoples for being like the Amalekites, who did not fear God (Deut 25:18), rather than like Gerar, which did (Gen 20:11).

Egregious Injustice

Egregious injustice is the other sin these prophetic oracles highlight. It is not that the people the oracles single out for condemnation have done *some* wrong to others, but that they have done excessively brutal things. Again, Isaiah's words against Babylon illustrate this point: The Lord brings judgment against "the scepter of rulers, that struck the peoples in wrath with unceasing blows, that ruled the nations in anger with unrelenting persecution" (Isa 14:5–6). Magistrates driven by anger will obviously tend toward immoderate behavior, an especially dangerous tendency for powerful people. It is not surprising, then, to read that they strike others with *unceasing* blows and rule with *unrelenting* persecution. Reading this, we get the sense that it is the excessive character of what they do that draws God's special attention.

One of the most interesting sets of oracles against Gentile nations appears in Amos 1:3–2:4, where God addresses six of Israel's close neighbors. Each of these oracles begins with the same introductory formula and then presents a distinctive charge. Each charge focuses on an injustice done to others, and all these injustices unsettle readers by their excessively brutal or unrelenting character. This text thus provides an excellent example of the point we are considering.

The first oracle condemns Damascus, for it "threshed Gilead with threshing sledges of iron" (Amos 1:3). While this is probably metaphorical, it creates a startling image in readers' minds. Threshing grain with iron sledges was a violent process, and whatever Damascus did to Gilead must have been brutal.[3] The next oracle turns to the Philistine city of Gaza, which "carried into exile a whole people to deliver them up to Edom" (1:6). This may refer to slave-trading, which is heinous enough, but the fact that Gaza did this to a *whole people* gives it an over-the-top character. It sounds like genocide. Amos then turns to Tyre, which "delivered up a whole people to Edom, and did not remember the covenant of brotherhood" (1:9). This takes Gaza's sins to a new level of excessiveness. Tyre not only delivered over a *whole people* but also broke a covenant. This likely refers to an oath-bound political treaty that binds two groups together and thus makes them like brothers. To

---

[3] Many commentators discuss this. E.g., see Francis I. Andersen and David Noel Freedman, *Amos: A New Translation with Introduction and Commentary* (New York: Doubleday, 1989), 239; and Hans Walter Wolff, *Joel and Amos*, trans. Waldemar Janzen, S. Dean McBride, and Charles A Muenchow (Philadelphia: Fortress, 1977), 154.

hand over *any* entire people group to slavery is horrible, but to break a treaty to do so is all the worse. It shows no fear of God, since oaths were sworn in God's name.

The fourth oracle targets Edom, which is really no surprise since Edom was a partner to the crimes of Gaza and Tyre. Edom "pursued his brother with the sword and cast off all pity, and his anger tore perpetually, and he kept his wrath forever" (1:11). Edom's assault against a *brother* is especially notable. We cannot be sure whether this was a brother created by covenant, as in the previous oracle, or a brother through common ancestors (which is what Israel was to Edom, since both descended from Abraham). Either way, the close relation of Edom to its victim exacerbates the wickedness of their deed. Furthermore, Edom went over the top, without constraint. It despised *all* pity and was angry *perpetually, forever*. Fifth, Amos speaks of the Ammonites, who "ripped open pregnant women in Gilead, that they might enlarge their border" (1:13). While the earlier imagery of a threshing sledge at least left something to the imagination, this oracle tells us exactly what the Ammonites did, and we can hardly bear to think about it. Targeting civilians in warfare is bad enough, but targeting the most vulnerable in such a horrible way, and all for the sake of a border dispute, astounds us. Finally, our old friend Moab comes back into view. Moab "burned to lime the bones of the king of Edom" (2:1). This does not sound as bad as what Ammon did, but desecrating the dead elicits outrage in almost every civilization. It serves no purpose other than to insult, dishonor, and provoke.

Bad things happen in the world. But we learn to live with most of them, however regrettable, and they cease to surprise us. Yet some things are so bad that they shock us and arouse our indignation. These are the sorts of things Amos and other prophets emphasized when denouncing Gentile nations. To borrow again words from the previous chapter, the prophets condemned them for doing things that make us say: "that just ought not to be done."

Natural Law in the Oracles

None of these Old Testament prophetic oracles mentions "natural law" by name, but what we have just seen leaves little doubt that natural law is very much in the background. These Gentile nations had perpetrated unspeakable atrocities, raising their fists to heaven and abusing their fellow humans without restraint. Their actions were not accidents or peccadillos. God treats them as if they knew what they were doing, and thus he pronounces judgment against them.

Where did their moral knowledge come from? It did not come from the Mosaic law, which God delivered to Israel alone. Our text in Amos makes this clear in an interesting way. After the six oracles against Gentile communities, Amos delivered oracles against Judah and Israel (2:4–16). Amos never mentioned the Mosaic law when addressing the Gentiles, but the first charge he brought against Judah was that "they have rejected the law of the LORD, and have not kept his statutes" (2:4). Israelites had the Mosaic law, and God would judge them for breaking it. But God would judge the Gentiles on some other basis. Unless we wish to indulge in some wild speculation that God specially revealed a set of laws to all these Gentile nations, the natural law must have been their source of knowledge. As observed in chapter 2, the Old Testament prophets believed that the natural order is purposeful and meaningful. We can hardly be surprised that they thought this natural order provided moral knowledge sufficient to hold all people liable to divine judgment.

These oracles are not meant to show that every human community that passes a certain threshold of wickedness will suffer

swift retaliation at God's hands. The oracles themselves never say
this. God brings "princes to nothing" (Isa 40:23), yet when and
how is mysterious. But these oracles do remind us that God sees
and cares what the rulers of this earth do. On the last day, he'll call
all of them to account for everything they have done, but sometimes there is also a reckoning amid history. When Christians suffer
and see others suffer at tyrants' hands, they can take heart that God
has an eye on these tyrants and will not let them plead ignorance
for their atrocities.

Divine Judgment and Natural Law in Romans 1–2

Natural law lay behind the scenes in the prophetic oracles against
Gentile nations. In Rom 1:18–2:16, Paul brings natural law to center stage. All the biblical writers we are considering in this chapter
sought to show that God holds *all* people accountable to his judgment, Gentiles as well as Jews. With the Old Testament prophets,
we are compelled to conclude that natural law is the only thing that
can explain this. But Paul tells us explicitly that God's law revealed
in nature is what summons all people before God's judgment and
ensures God's justice in condemning them. Biblical scholars have
had numerous debates about these texts, although there is no space
to interact with them here.[4] There are good reasons, however, why
most Christian theologians through history have regarded Rom
1:18–2:16 as powerful testimony to God's universal judgment on
the basis of natural law.

---

[4] For detailed discussion about many of these debates, and my interaction with them, see DCMO, chap. 5.

The introductory section of Romans ends with 1:17, in which Paul quotes one of his favorite Old Testament verses, Hab 2:4: "The righteous shall live by faith." Then Paul begins a new section in 1:18, which continues all the way through 3:20, before he again picks up the theme of righteousness by faith in 3:21–22. In this lengthy intervening section, Paul provides crucial background for his gospel of salvation through faith in Christ. I'll come back to the importance of 1:18–3:20 as *background* material at the end of this chapter. For now, let's look at the opening two parts of this text and consider how they speak about natural law.

Romans 1:18–32

God's judgment against sin is front and center in this text. Paul begins by stating that "the wrath of God is revealed from heaven against all ungodliness and unrighteousness of men, who by their unrighteousness suppress the truth" (1:18). This raises some of the same issues that the prophetic oracles did: If God's wrath is coming against *all* unrighteousness, then all people must know God's moral requirements. Only then can he justly hold them responsible for breaking them. Paul agreed with this and wanted to explain how it works.

In 1:19 Paul wrote, "For what can be known about God is plain to them, because God has shown it to them." This is striking. Knowledge of God is not possible or obscure. It is *plain*. It is plain because God himself has shown it to them. How does he do so, we wonder? "For his invisible attributes, namely, his eternal power and divine nature, have been clearly perceived, ever since the creation of the world, in the things that have been made" (1:20). Here Scripture puts *natural revelation* before us as clearly as it ever does: God *shows* his existence and character to all people *through the things he has created.* But just how plain is this natural revelation? Plain enough that those who receive it "are without excuse" (1:20), for those who refuse to honor God "knew God" (1:21). God is just in judging all people because all people know and are accountable to him through natural revelation. These verses assure us that everything we thought must be true when reading the prophetic oracles is in fact true.

The following verses (1:21–28) further explain the dynamic of what Paul has just introduced: God reveals himself in nature, people know him and ought to respond well, but they rebel instead and act "contrary to nature" (1:26). Therefore, God "gave them up" to still further acts of rebellion (1:24, 26, 28). Paul then declares that they are "filled with all manner of unrighteousness" and issues a long list of sins to illustrate his point (1:29–31). The final verse is a fitting conclusion: "Though they know God's righteous decree that those who practice such things deserve to die, they not only do them but give approval to those who practice them" (1:32). Once again, Paul says that they *know* what is true. But there is a new wrinkle here as well. They do not merely know that certain behavior is morally wrong; they know that those engaging in these actions *deserve to die.* That is, they know that these rebellious acts against natural revelation justly bring divine judgment. They suppress it, and they approve of others who suppress it, but they know it.

Romans 2:1–16

There is a transition at 2:1. Paul has been explaining things in general, referring to wicked people as "they" and "them." Then suddenly he points his finger at readers: "Therefore you have no excuse, O man, every one of you who judges. For in passing judgment on another you condemn yourself, because you, the judge, practice the very same things" (2:1). Perhaps he was thinking primarily here of Jews after focusing on Gentiles in the previous verses. (He at least turns to Jewish readers at 2:17.) In any case, Paul wanted to be sure that no one would feel safe from God's judgment when he looks at his own life. We can imagine readers who see Paul condemn those who *give approval* to evildoers in 1:32 and think to themselves, *Well, I don't approve of such people.* Paul seems to address such readers when he says that those who *pass judgment* on evildoers are also without excuse (like the evildoers themselves in 1:20). The reason is hypocrisy: they do the same sorts of things as the evildoers they condemn. The noose of divine judgment tightens.

At this transition point, Paul's emphasis clearly falls on what people "practice." He used this term in 1:32 and 2:1, and then he used it twice more, thus using it four verses in a row: "We know that the judgment of God rightfully falls on those who practice such things. Do you suppose, O man—you who judge those who practice such things and yet do them yourself—that you will escape the judgment of God?" (2:2–3). Paul's chief point is that God's judgment is coming against *all* who practice evil works. People can concoct lots of rationalizations and create various diversions in hope of being judged on some other basis. But God's judgment is straightforward and impartial. He'll judge everyone on the basis of what he does. (Paul later explains how to escape this terrifying prospect through faith in Christ, but he needed to lay this foundation first.)

Paul wanted to leave no question about his meaning. He adds, "[God] will render to each one according to his works: to those who by patience in well-doing seek for glory and honor and immorality, he will give eternal life; but for those who are self-seeking and do not obey the truth, but obey unrighteousness, there will be wrath and fury" (2:6–8). Again, his judgment is according to what people practice. Nothing else matters. Perhaps at least it matters whether one is a Jew or a Gentile? No, not even that: "There will be tribulation and distress for every human being who does evil, the Jew first and also the Greek, but glory and honor and peace for everyone who does good, the Jew first and also the Greek" (2:9–10). That sure sounds impartial, which Paul confirms: "God shows no partiality" (2:11).

This flattening out of the spiritual status of Jews and Gentiles before God's judgment may trigger again that persistent question: How can this be, since God gave his specially revealed law to Israel but not to others? As in Romans 1, Paul was again keen to answer. In the next verse he wrote, "For all who have sinned without the law will also perish without the law; and all who have sinned under the law will be judged by the law" (2:12). This sounds exactly right, as far as it goes. God will only judge people by the law if he has given them the law. That is what our instincts tell us, and Paul confirms. But then Paul seems to have complicated things, or perhaps even contradicted himself: "For it is not the hearers of the law who are righteous before God, but the doers of the law who will be justified" (2:13). On one level this simply reiterates the earlier statements about God's impartiality in judging everyone strictly by what they practice. (We should keep in mind that to be *justified* is to be declared righteous, which is an act of judgment.) But how can justification be possible only by doing *the law* when Paul has just said that those who do not have the law will not be judged by it? It would seem that the only way Paul can extract himself from this corner is by explaining that there is a way to *do the law* even if one does not have the (Mosaic) law.

This is precisely what he does in the next verses, and the natural law is what brings everything together: "For when Gentiles, who do not have the law, by nature do what the law requires, they are a law to themselves, even though they do not have the law. They show that the work of the law is written on their hearts, while their conscience also bears witness, and their conflicting thoughts accuse or even excuse them" (2:14–15). Gentiles do not have the Mosaic law, but they still have a way to do what this law requires. That is not because God specially revealed his moral will to them on a mountain other than Sinai through someone other than Moses. It is because *the work of the law* is written on their hearts, and their consciences bear witness to it. They are thus a kind of *law to themselves*. Both when these Gentiles do what is right (and their consciences "excuse" them) and when they do what is wrong (and their consciences "accuse" them), they are responding to God's law and the righteousness it reveals. Thus, Jews and Gentiles really are in the same boat, though they embarked in different ways. God will judge all people impartially according to whatever version of his law they have access to. So indeed, only the doers of the law will be justified.

The Rest of Romans 1:18–3:20

We will not look in detail at the rest of this first main section of Romans. But we should keep in mind Paul's main point, in preparation for what we will consider next. Paul is helpful in telling us exactly what his main point is: "We have already charged that all, both Jews and Greeks, are under sin" (3:9). Of course, not everyone commits all the sins listed in Romans 1, and Gentiles' consciences sometimes excuse rather than accuse them (2:15), but no one is righteous all the time. All are sinners. "None is righteous, no, not one" (3:10). When it comes down to it, ultimately, "There is no fear of God before their eyes" (3:18). Thus, "by works of the law no human being will be justified" in God's sight (3:20). Doers of the law will be justified (2:13), yes, but there is no one who meets that standard.

We should not let the Abimelechs or Egyptian midwives of the world fool us, as if doing some noble deeds under the influence of natural law gives anyone hope of escaping God's judgment forever. Thus, our study of natural law in Rom 1:18–3:20 ends on an incredibly sobering note.

Natural Law and the Gospel of Christ

But just when Paul has taken readers to this low point, he begins the next section of Romans with two of the best little words ever written: "But now . . ." (3:21). He then explains that though there is no hope for anyone of being justified by doing the law, God has offered justification to all people through faith in Christ, a justification of the *ungodly* (4:5) through the forgiveness of sins and the imputation of Christ's righteousness (4:6–8; 5:15–19). The accountability of all people before God's impartial judgment is an important Christian doctrine in its own right, but Paul's purpose in Rom 1:18–3:20 is to lay a foundation for the gospel of salvation at the center of Christian faith and life. And since natural law is a crucial part of Rom 1:18–3:20, natural law must be part of that gospel foundation.

In this final section of the chapter, I suggest four related ways in which the natural law provides a foundation for the gospel of Christ. The first three come directly from Romans, and the final one draws on broader concerns of this book.

First, natural law is a crucial foundation for the gospel because it exposes the sin of all people, particularly those who do not have the Mosaic law. It is important to ask why Paul did not move straight from Rom 1:17 to the explanation of the gospel he began in 3:21. Why take the route through such rough terrain? The basic answer is that the Christian gospel is incomprehensible for people who feel secure in their own good works. The gospel is for the condemned and miserable. As mentioned previously, it is a message for the *ungodly* (4:5). It announces reconciliation with God by faith *rather than* works (e.g., 4:4–5; 10:32). It offers the righteousness of Christ *instead of* our own righteousness through the law (e.g., 10:3; Phil 3:9). The Mosaic law does some of the heavy lifting in preparing the way for the gospel: "Whatever the law says it speaks to those who are under the law, so that every mouth may be stopped, and the whole world may be held accountable to God" (Rom 3:19). Or as Paul puts it in Galatians, all who are of the works of the law "are under a curse; for it is written, 'Cursed be everyone who does not abide by all things written in the Book of the Law, and do them'" (Gal 3:10). But we have seen in Rom 1:18–3:20 that natural law plays the same function. It exposes sin and takes away self-confidence, both prerequisites for understanding the good news.

Second, and closely related, natural law helps to secure the unity of Jews and Gentiles in Christ, which was a difficult and contentious issue in the church's earliest days. Romans 1:18–3:20 acknowledges that Jewish people had many spiritual privileges (3:1–2), and they knew it, although they often viewed these privileges as a cause for boasting (2:17–20). Theirs was "the adoption, the glory, the covenants, the giving of the law, the worship," "the promises," and "the patriarchs" (9:4–5). But now in Christ, God was opening the gates of heaven to Gentiles as well, on equal footing with the Jews. This dynamic emerges as a tension already in the Gospels (e.g., Matt 21:33–46), commands major attention in Acts (e.g., 10:1–11:18; 15:1–36; 21:17–26), and is a central theme of Galatians and Hebrews, as well as Romans. How could Gentiles be heirs of the same God and kingdom when Jews alone had the long

heritage of the Mosaic law, which had been Israel's unique posses-
sion for more than a millennium? The way the New Testament
resolves this issue involves a bigger explanation than I can provide
here. For now, I simply note that natural law is one piece of that
puzzle. Romans 1:18–3:20 shows that the Mosaic law and natural
law teach the same basic righteous standard and that both leave the
people it addresses unable to claim confidence in their own works
before God's judgment. Whatever unique blessings Jews had, Jews
and Gentiles hear the gospel of Christ with the same legal message
echoing in their ears.

The third issue extends this thought a bit further. As Paul
developed the doctrine of salvation in Romans, one way he spoke
of justification was in terms of dying to the law or being released
from the law (Rom 7:4, 6). In context, Paul's immediate reference is clearly the law of Moses (7:7–13). Describing justification
as death to or release from the Mosaic law makes sense in a way,
since Israel constantly transgressed that law and thereby fell under
God's curse. Israel needed to be rescued from that, for sure. But this
brings us back to the issue of Gentiles' place in God's plan of salvation. The Gentiles were never under the Mosaic law and did not
need to be released from its condemnation. There does not seem
to be any relevance for them of a justification that promises release
from something that was never their problem. But here we remember what Paul has already explained about the natural law. Natural
law put Gentiles in the same spiritual predicament as the Mosaic
law put Israel: in need of rescue from divine judgment. Paul could
describe justification in terms of Israel's release from the Mosaic law
because Israel's problem under Moses showcased the problem of the
whole world. Gentile readers of Romans should see themselves in
how Paul described Israel's problem and deliverance. The reality of
natural law makes this possible.

The final issue concerns broader matters we have already explored in this book. Christianity teaches that God made the first creation *ex nihilo*—out of nothing. Christianity also teaches the hope of a new creation, but God will not bring about that new creation *ex nihilo*. The new creation was the goal and destiny of the first creation all along (see, for example, Heb 2:5–10). Christ does not create a new group of human beings to populate his everlasting kingdom but redeems existing humans. Paul touches on these issues in Romans when he refers to the fallen creation groaning and looking forward to the glorious resurrection of believers (Rom 8:18–25). The reality of natural law is one proof that this world is not fallen beyond repair. If the world were nothing but a sea of meaningless, purposeless chaos, there would be nothing from which God could rebuild. If human beings had no rationality or understanding, there would be no image-bearers for God to redeem. The enduring meaning, purpose, and order of this world, expressed in the natural law, is another foundational element of the gospel of Christ.

5

Natural Law in the Christian Life

T hus far, this book has considered natural law from the perspective of Christian theology, but it has not focused on the
place of natural law within the Christian life itself. We have considered the importance of natural law for a doctrine of creation, for
God's preservation of the fallen world and human societies, and
even for laying a foundation for the gospel. But does natural law
have any importance for how Christians live day by day? This chapter argues that natural law matters a great deal and seeks to show
how it is indispensable for faithful Christian living.

Another way to think about this is in terms of the *three uses
of the law*, as understood in classical Reformation theology.[1] In its
first use, God's law shows people their sin and exposes their need

---

[1] See also a summary in Louis Berkhof, *Systematic Theology*, 4th ed.
(Grand Rapids: Eerdmans, 1993), 614–15. Berkhof and some other writers reverse the order of the first and second uses as described below.

for a savior. In its second use, the law serves to promote justice and constrain wickedness in our civil societies. Previous chapters have reflected at some length on how natural law functions in these first two ways. In its third use, the law serves as a guide for Christians, to show them how to pursue gratefully obedient lives in Christ. God's law revealed in Scripture clearly promotes this use, but we have not yet inquired whether the natural law does as well. This chapter seeks to show that it most certainly does.

Before we explore how the natural moral order continues to guide and obligate Christians, it is important to note its limits as well. In many respects, Christians are to live in ways that go beyond and even confound the natural law. As citizens of heaven (Phil 3:20) called to set their minds on the things above rather than on earthly things (Col 3:2), Christians have moral responsibilities the world cannot understand. To mention just two examples: the New Testament exhorts us to love and forgive each other as God in Christ has loved and forgiven us (e.g., Eph 4:32–5:2; 1 John 3:16; 4:11), and it calls us to give extravagantly to each other as Christ gave himself extravagantly for us (2 Cor 8:1–9). These exhortations portray a way of life that far transcends the moral insight we gain through knowing and experiencing the present world. This is an extremely important issue in Christian ethics, but we will not consider it further here since it concerns matters other than natural law.[2]

To explain the crucial role that natural law does play in the Christian life, this chapter will first return to the book of Proverbs and consider its teaching from this new angle. Then we will move to the New Testament. In both subtle and explicit ways, Jesus and his apostles indicate that much of the Christian life is far from

---

[2] But see DCMO, 430–76. At more length, see also RMT, part 1.

innovative but reflects the basic obligations of the natural law. Issues of marriage and the church's care for her pastors provide concrete examples.

Natural Law and the Christian Life in Proverbs

Previous chapters have spent time in Proverbs because Proverbs primarily describes how people gain wisdom through observing and contemplating how this world works. It treats the world as meaningful, purposeful, and orderly. Proverbs helps us see that there are fitting and unfitting ways for creatures like us to live in this world.

These truths remain important for what follows. But here we also want to take seriously how God inspired the book of Proverbs *for his redeemed covenant people.* He gave Proverbs not to the Moabites or Babylonians, but to Israel. So, although Proverbs provides insight as to how unbelievers gain moral knowledge from the natural order, its chief purpose was to help believers themselves navigate wisely through everyday life. New-covenant Christians have no less need for wisdom than the Israelites did.[3] Jesus told his disciples to be wise as serpents (Matt 10:16), for example, and Paul calls readers to live as the wise do and make the best use of their time (Eph 5:15–16). The New Testament does not include a book like Proverbs, and the reason seems clear: Christ's redemptive work did not change the natural law, and insofar as believers need help in acquiring wisdom through the natural order, Proverbs continues to

---

[3] The "new covenant" refers to God's covenant relationship with his church between Christ's death and his second coming, as described in Jeremiah 31, Luke 22, 2 Corinthians 3, and Hebrews 8, for example.

give us what we need. What follows explores some ways in which
this is true.

Natural Law and Things Scripture Does Not Address

First, natural law is necessary for guiding Christians in areas of life
Scripture does not address, and Proverbs instructs us how to gain
this natural-law knowledge. Consider the Mosaic law. As extensive
as it was, it did not address many aspects of morality and civil law.[4]
What were Israelites supposed to do when dealing with these areas
of life, and how were their judges supposed to resolve disputes about
them? If they did not have a general knowledge of the natural law,
it is difficult to see how they could make objective decisions about
these things in ways they could explain persuasively to one another.

One way to appreciate this point is by recognizing that the
Mosaic law made use of *case law*. Instead of simply giving long lists
of rules, it gives examples of how to resolve certain kinds of disputes
by providing a relatively small number of concrete examples, which
Israelites were then to apply to similar cases that were not addressed.
Such case law would be completely unhelpful without natural law.
How is a person supposed to know how to make analogies from
a specific case to different life situations? If one spots a similarity
between a concrete biblical case and a real-life situation, how does
one know if it is a *relevant* similarity for purposes of doing what is

---

[4] For discussion, see, e.g., Jonathan Burnside, *God, Justice, and Society:
Aspects of Law and Legality in the Bible* (Oxford: Oxford University Press,
2011), 18–20. Burnside notes several biblical stories in which Israelites
asked Moses for help resolving cases—concerning blasphemy, impurity,
gathering wood on the Sabbath, and inheritance for women—because the
law didn't provide instruction (Lev 24:10–23; Num 9:6–14; 15:32–36;
and 27:1–11).

just? The Mosaic law itself did not include an instruction manual for these sorts of judgments. Here is a simple illustration. Imagine that someone passes by on the road near an Israelite's property, and the latter's dog leaps out of the bushes and mauls the traveler to death. The authorities investigate the case and cannot find anything in the Mosaic law that says what to do when a dog kills a person. So, one person proposes Exod 21:12–14 as an applicable analogy: If one man strikes another to death, he should die. However, if it was not premeditated but a matter of providential circumstances out of his control, he may flee to a city of refuge and be spared from vengeance. Since the dog certainly did not make any plans to ambush this traveler, it should be sent to a city of refuge. But then another person proposes Exod 21:28–32 as a better analogy: in the case of an ox that gores a person to death, the ox should be killed, and its owner should be held responsible if he knew that his ox was prone to do such a thing. Which analogy is better?

It may seem like a ridiculous question because the latter example strikes us as much more appropriate. But how do we know this? We know it because we understand important facts about the world and how it works. We understand that treating human beings justly demands taking account of their intentions because humans have reason and will and need to be judged accordingly. We understand that asking whether a dog planned and carried out a murder is nonsensical, for dogs cannot act in that manner. For all the differences between an ox and a dog, they are much more like each other than either one is like a human being. In short, we understand some basic but important things about how the world works and its implications for living in just and peaceful ways. The Mosaic law *presumed* that Israelites reading the law would understand these things. It relied on their preexisting perception of natural revelation when providing the sort of case law that it did.

The New Testament does not provide civil laws as the Old Testament did, because the church is not a political community as Israel in Canaan was. But it does give all sorts of instruction about how Christians should conduct themselves. Yet here again there are many life issues the New Testament has nothing to say about. One Christian is trying to figure out the best employees to hire for her small business. Another is striving to be a good math teacher. Both will be in trouble if they do not understand how the world works and perceive its moral implications. Of course, the New Testament delineates plenty of general rules to follow in these and other circumstances: be impartial, be kind, be compassionate, and so forth. But these, too, depend deeply on an understanding of the world around us. How effective and edifying will a well-meaning Christian be if she is clueless about how human beings ordinarily respond to certain sorts of words and actions? Is a Christian being impartial if he treats a blind person exactly the same way he treats someone with 20/20 vision? Might Christian kindness and compassion demand different responses to different people—say, one employee who is late to work because his child vomited right before he was leaving home and another who is late because she was awake most of the night getting drunk? Christians can have impartial, kind, or compassionate intentions but do all sorts of harm if they are unfamiliar with the ways of the world.

How is Proverbs relevant in light of such facts? As mentioned in chapter 2, Proverbs reminds us of things we must do to gain this acquaintance with the world and its moral implications, things Christians can easily forget: Be alert. Open your eyes. Pay attention to what is going on around you. Look, and then reflect on what you have observed. There is ultimately no substitute for such deliberation if we want to understand human interaction and natural cause and effect and, thus, if we want to be effective in putting our good intentions into practice. We will consider these things further in chapter 6.

Natural Law and Things Scripture Does Address

Natural law is crucial for dealing well with moral issues Scripture does not explicitly address, but it is also important for dealing with issues Scripture *does* address. The wisdom we gain from observing and reflecting on the natural moral order is not useful simply for filling in gaps where Scripture is silent. This is obvious once we recognize that the rest of Scripture is not silent about most moral issues Proverbs discusses. The Bible issues many commands against adultery, laziness, drunkenness, fits of rage, and cruel use of the tongue, but Proverbs frequently treats these sins from the perspective of natural law.

The reason for this is that God wants Christians to understand something deeper about the moral life than simply that God has commanded this or prohibited that. Of course, the fact that God has commanded or prohibited something is good enough reason to do or not do it. But God also desires that Christians understand *why* he commands and prohibits what he does. God's law often reads as it does because some conduct runs with the grain of the universe and other conduct cuts against it. Proverbs helps us see this. It startles us into realizing that our sins are stupid and destructive. They make us look like idiots to other people. Proverbs exposes sin for all its folly. If Christians wish to comprehend the moral life deeply—with insight and understanding—it is important that we understand this.

Sometimes it takes seeing the absurdity of sin as a violation of the natural order to rouse Christians out of foolish patterns of behavior. If we look honestly at our own and other Christians' conduct, it is amazing to realize how many things we do—and keep doing—that make our own and others' lives miserable, unproductive, and unsatisfying. Despite all the spiritual blessings we have in Christ, we often persist in behavior whose stupidity many pagans can readily recognize. Sometimes we need to see ourselves as others see us. To be clear, this is far from the only motivation Christians have for godly behavior, nor the most important. And it is not the case that acting according to the natural law always makes life great or that acting against it is always immediately destructive. We are thinking about patterns and tendencies, not a rigidly predictable cause-and-effect moral universe. Yet the point stands: if we are to comprehend how evil our sin is and be fully motivated to avoid it, we need to see it as utterly stupid as well as a violation of God's rules.

Adultery provides perhaps the best examples in Proverbs. Several texts in the prologue (chapters 1–9) present adultery as stupidity. As one verse puts it, "He who commits adultery lacks sense" (6:32). Proverbs assigns this verdict not only to the act of adultery itself but also to toying with it, putting oneself in tempting circumstances, and being captivated by someone who is not one's spouse. A man should not even "go near the door" of the "forbidden woman" but stay "far from her" (5:3, 8). He should not be "intoxicated" with her (5:20), "desire her beauty," or be captured "with her eyelashes" (6:25). Are such things against God's law? Yes. The seventh commandment forbids adultery, and the tenth commandment forbids coveting another's spouse. But Proverbs does not simply repeat rules; it helps us perceive what is behind them. Proverbs analogizes adultery to things in the natural world that are obviously ridiculous. Adultery is like having a well and letting its water run into the streets for others to take (5:15–17). It is like letting "strangers take their fill of your strength" (5:10). Who would do things so inane? It makes others look at you and say: "How dumb!" People do not despise a hungry person who steals food, but they do despise an adulterer, whose "disgrace will not be wiped away" (6:33).

Proverbs also emphasizes how destructive adultery is to one's own life. The person who is not one's spouse may have lips that "drip honey" and speech "smoother than oil, but in the end she is bitter as wormwood, sharp as a two-edged sword" (5:3–4). Other analogies from the natural world illustrate what adultery is like: "Can a man carry fire next to his chest and his clothes not be burned? Or can one walk on hot coals and his feet not be scorched?" (6:27–28). It is thus no wonder that adultery brings regret: "At the end of your life you groan, when your flesh and body are consumed, and you say, 'How I hated discipline, and my heart despised reproof! I did not listen to the voice of my teachers or incline my ear to my instructors. I am at the brink of utter ruin in the assembled congregation'" (5:11–14). Proverbs thus compels Christians who are tantalized by or harboring secret desires for individuals other than their spouses to ask themselves: *What in the world am I doing? Wouldn't I look ridiculous to someone who could see my thoughts? Why would I go down a path that threatens to ruin my life and fill me with shame and regret?*

The most striking text in Proverbs on this subject is the extended description of someone looking out his window and observing a young man, "simple" and "lacking sense," who gets seduced by an adulteress (7:6–23). The entire scene is designed to let readers see from a distance what folly it is to fall for such a person. It is so easy to see when looking at someone else, yet so difficult to see in ourselves. Proverbs thus pries us away from our own delusions and makes us look in the mirror to see ourselves as we really are. We can appreciate sin in its nonsensical madness only when we do.

Proverbs does this for many other moral issues too. Take laziness. Christians know they should work hard. But all believers are tempted to slack off at least once in a while, and many Christians struggle mightily with laziness day by day. To help us, Proverbs illustrates what laziness really is: it makes lazy people look ridiculous to anyone watching them objectively, and it brings trouble to their own lives. Consider a couple of adjacent proverbs about the sluggard: "As a door turns on its hinges, so does a sluggard on his bed. The sluggard buries his hand in the dish; it wears him out to bring it back to his mouth" (26:14–15). These proverbs are designed to make readers laugh. They hold lazy people before us and deride them. No one who reads these proverbs could possibly want to be the person depicted. Yet how many Christians play the sluggard? Proverbs also repeatedly warns about the poverty that laziness tends to bring. Thus, we also ask: What person would want to make himself poor? Yet so many Christians indulge behavior that leads directly to want. Laziness is not just a violation of biblical rules. It is dumb.

Or how about abuse of alcohol? The New Testament tells us not to get drunk (Eph 5:18), so it is hardly a difficult question whether alcohol abuse is contrary to God's law. But as with sex, so with alcohol: Christians often take a good gift from God and use it in harmful ways. They have heard the biblical commands but failed to see the reality of what they are doing. Proverbs says: "Wine is a mocker, strong drink a brawler, and whoever is led astray by it is not wise" (20:1). Letting alcohol get the best of us makes us a laughingstock and inspires us to mock and brawl with others. What person would be foolish enough to mess with this? Well, wine is attractive, like the forbidden woman. It "sparkles in the cup and goes down smoothly" (23:31). But it brings nothing but trouble to those who "tarry long" over it (23:30). It brings woe, sorrow, strife, complaining, wounds, and bloodshot eyes (23:29). It "bites like a serpent and stings like an adder" (23:32). It makes us see and say bizarre things (23:33). Who would do this to himself? "You will be like one who lies down in the midst of the sea, like one who lies on the top of a mast. 'They struck me,' you will say, 'but I was not hurt; they beat me, but I did not feel it. When shall I awake? I must have another drink'" (23:34–35). Who would want others to look at her and see this? Christians tempted to abuse alcohol need to perceive how it overturns the natural order, turning a divine image-bearer into a delirious babbler.

Finally, two other sins Proverbs treats similarly are worth considering: gossip and fits of anger. Scripture clearly prohibits these sins, leaving no doubt that they displease God. Yet Christians often indulge them. They sneak up on us unexpectedly, and we fall into them without thinking. Proverbs helps us see how destructive and undesirable these sins are. It shows us their reality.

Proverbs warns against gossip as it often warns about other sins, by offering analogies: "The words of a whisperer are like delicious morsels; they go down into the inner parts of the body" (18:8). There is something inherently powerful about gossip. People delight in it and take it in like good food. Ironically, this imagery is revolting. What sort of a person would willingly devour something disgusting or something that would tear up one's insides? But this is the reality of gossip. It destroys friendships (16:28; 17:9). A gossiper does not just lose the friendship of people he gossips about but also loses the friendship of sensible people who know his reputation as a gossiper and do not want to fall victim to his words (20:19). And no one wants to lose his friends. Furthermore, avoiding quarrels is as easy as avoiding fires: Take away the wood, no more fire. Take away the gossip, no more quarrel (26:20). Yet how easy, even for Christians, to get sucked into the momentary delight of sharing or hearing what ought to be kept secret. Proverbs helps us see gossip for what it really is.

Finally, Christians know they should not let the sun go down on their anger (Eph 4:26), but anger can be so difficult to keep under control when things do not go exactly right. Proverbs shows us anger in its raw reality. In some texts, Proverbs speaks of rage as an instigator of folly (e.g., 14:17, 29). Where there is a short temper, sin is sure to follow. Anger is like drunkenness: a person basically loses his mind, and you just never know what he'll do or say. Whatever the angry person's action, we can be sure he "stirs up strife" (15:18; 29:22). A hot temper makes a person less than human and destroys peace in the community. Who would want to see a video of herself during a temper tantrum? Once again, Proverbs helps us see that sin does more than break a rule. Sin fights against the nature of things. It is disordered, destructive, and stupid.

Natural Law and the Christian Life in the New Testament

There is nothing in the New Testament that draws upon natural law to explain the Christian life in quite the way we have just seen in Proverbs. Nevertheless, the natural moral order remains in the background throughout New Testament instruction on life in Christ. On several occasions, New Testament writers appeal to it specially to make an important moral point. The rest of the chapter turns to this New Testament material.

The Conservative Nature of New Testament Ethics

As mentioned at the beginning of this chapter, there are many distinctive characteristics of the Christian moral life presented in the New Testament. Christ's death and resurrection atoned for his people's sins and inaugurated the kingdom of God, and there are profound implications for Christians' moral life. Yet there is also something fundamentally conservative about New Testament ethics. By that, I mean that much of what the New Testament commands and prohibits is not new at all. It reaffirms what we already know, things that were morally obligatory long before Christ came. We should worship God alone, honor our parents, and refrain from adultery, stealing, and lying, and numerous other familiar things.

When we think about the conservative nature of New Testament ethics, it is a reminder that many New Testament commands are not true *because* the New Testament commands them. Rather, the New Testament commands created actions because they are true. This does not mean that morality is ever independent of God. It is God who made the world and made human beings in the way he did. He established the natural law, which reflects his own holiness. Because God and human nature have not changed, the natural law remains an abiding presence for the New Testament Christian life, even when not mentioned by name.

This may also help us when considering seemingly important issues that the New Testament does not treat. The issue of justice is a glaring example. Though the Old Testament says much about justice, the Christian who looks to the New Testament for instruction about how to resolve cases in court or even for exhortations to pursue justice in their societies will struggle to find a single clear example.[5]

---

[5] I realize that many readers will be surprised at this claim, but it's true. Some writers find a call for justice in biblical commands to be attentive to the poor; e.g., Timothy Keller, *Generous Justice: How God's Grace Makes Us Just* (New York: Dutton, 2010), 2, 5, 43, 56–57, 101–8, 177. But while the New Testament indeed calls Christians to be kind and generous to the poor, it never calls for political action to help them. Some writers also

Does this mean Christians should not vote or hold political office or support good causes in the public square? Not if natural law remains in the background. The New Testament had good reason to be silent about whether and how to pursue justice. Most early Christians did not possess civil authority, and the Roman political system did not offer ordinary people opportunity to participate in political deliberations. Perhaps more important is that the new-covenant church should not exercise civil power, unlike Israel under the Mosaic law. The New Testament thus needed to train new-covenant Christians for life in a kingdom not of this world (John 18:36) and for citizenship in heaven (Phil 3:20), which are far more important than provisional affairs of state. But some Christians live in political environments that offer opportunities to hold office or contribute to public-policy debates. Because the New Testament affirms the continuing authority of natural law, Christians can be confident that political participation is a valid way to serve one's neighbors. They can also be confident that the standard of justice they seek is the same one that unbelievers know through natural revelation.

Back to the Created Order: Marriage

Therefore, natural law abides in the background of New Testament ethics. But there are also times when the New Testament sends us

---

appeal to the fact that the Greek word *dikaiosune*, which is usually translated as "righteousness," can also be translated as "justice." E.g., Nicholas Wolterstorff, *Justice: Rights and Wrongs* (Princeton: Princeton University Press, 2008), chap. 5. This is true, but when the New Testament uses this word in exhortations to Christians (which it doesn't often), there is not a single instance when it's clear that it should be translated "justice" and several instances when it clearly should not be translated this way.

back to the natural law directly. Let's consider two examples to conclude the chapter. The first comes from Jesus's teaching on marriage and divorce, and the second from Paul's reflections on how the church should treat its ministers.

The opening of Matthew 19 records a confrontation between Jesus and the Pharisees. The Pharisees ask Jesus a simple question: "Is it lawful to divorce one's wife for any cause?" (19:3). But behind the simplicity of their question is an important issue with potentially huge ramifications for family life. The Jewish community of Jesus's day was divided on this matter, which made the Pharisees' inquiry all the more dramatic. The crowd that was present (19:2) must have wondered how Jesus would interpret the Mosaic law and whose side he would take in their rabbis' debate.

But as so often happened in situations like these, Jesus defied expectations and responded on his own terms, not on those of the people who challenged him. Throughout Matthew, Jesus characteristically resolves difficult moral issues not by proving what the Mosaic law taught but by explaining how his followers are to live now that he has come and the kingdom of heaven has drawn near. Often this meant new and better practices that reflect Christ's accomplishment of the salvation that godly Israelites of old were expecting but had not yet seen.[6] But here, with the question of divorce, Jesus pointed his Jewish listeners not *beyond* the Mosaic law to its fulfillment in him but *before* the Mosaic law, to what God did in creation. There are new ways of looking at family under the new covenant, as the very next text in Matthew 19 indicates (19:10–12). When it comes to divorce, however, Christians should simply adhere to the created order, which we see in Jesus's explanation.

---

[6] See RMT, chap. 2.

His response to the Pharisees begins, "Have you not read that he who created them from the beginning made them male and female, and said, 'Therefore a man shall leave his father and his mother and hold fast to his wife, and the two shall become one flesh'?" (19:4–5). Although Jesus quoted from Scripture (Gen 2:24), he actually engaged in natural-law reasoning. He quoted Scripture as evidence of what marriage is by nature: an intimate union of one man and one woman. His next words draw a moral conclusion from the nature of marriage: "So they are no longer two but one flesh. What therefore God has joined together, let not man separate" (Matt 19:6). This is natural-law reasoning in the classical sense described in chapter 1. Jesus recognizes that the nature of a thing and its moral purpose are inseparable. From the divinely established one-flesh nature of marriage, therefore, he concludes that it ought not to be broken.

Jesus thus appealed to the natural law to resolve a moral con-troversy that the Pharisees thought had to be resolved through the Mosaic law. The Pharisees themselves were confused about this, for they asked next, alluding to Deut 24:1: "Why then did Moses com-mand one to give a certificate of divorce and to send her away?" (19:7).[7] That the Pharisees had been looking to the Mosaic law for answers was not wrong. Until this point, they had lived under the old covenant, and the Mosaic law was their prime, God-given moral standard. But Jesus was not interested in resolving disputes about how things were supposed to work under the old covenant. He wished to show how his covenant people were to live in the

---

[7] Deuteronomy 24:1 doesn't in fact *command* anyone to give his wife a certificate of divorce and send her away. It simply describes what ought to happen in certain circumstances *if* a man does these things, as the larger context (24:1–4) makes clear.

new age he was ushering in. We can see this in Jesus's next words, in response to the Pharisees' question about Moses: "Because of your hardness of heart Moses allowed you to divorce your wives, but from the beginning it was not so" (19:8). Jesus spoke about the Mosaic law as something binding in the past, but whose expiration date had arrived. God's people need to adhere to the natural law and no longer view rupture of the marriage union as "permissible."

Jesus's words may be troubling. Do they suggest that the Mosaic law contradicts the natural law? If the Mosaic law is God's law and is thus holy, righteous, and good, as Paul put it (Rom 7:12), how could it permit something fundamentally immoral, contrary to the natural order? Jesus's emphasis upon *permission* should alleviate this concern. The Mosaic law never prohibited divorce or established punishments for it, but that is quite different from *approving* of divorce. The Mosaic law was good and righteous *for the situation of old-covenant Israel.* No civil law code in this fallen world can prohibit and punish every sin or try to right every wrong. All civil law must be accommodated to the circumstances and weaknesses of the people it governs, as the Christian tradition has long recognized.[8] The Mosaic law also did this for Israel, according to the perfect wisdom of God who gave it. It may be that our civil law today should also permit divorce because of hardness of heart, for it is difficult to believe that people in our present political communities, which are not in redemptive covenant with God, have less hard hearts than God's old-covenant people. In any case, new-covenant Christians should live by the higher standard of the natural law.

Jesus's response to the Pharisees' second question included one more verse, which is worth a brief comment. He said, "And I say

---

[8] For two examples, see Thomas Aquinas, *Summa Theologiae* 1a2ae 95.3; and John Calvin, *Institutes of the Christian Religion*, 4.20.16.

to you: whoever divorces his wife, except for sexual immorality, and marries another, commits adultery" (19:9). Here, Jesus alerts us that the no-divorce rule is not absolute. Many general moral rules have exceptions, so in itself this is not troubling. But Jesus did not explain why sexual infidelity justifies divorce (and remarriage) for the wronged spouse.[9] If we think in natural-law terms, however, the reason becomes apparent. If one's spouse has committed adultery, he or she has already ruptured the one-flesh marriage union. Thus, divorcing such a person does not violate the "let not man separate" command, but formalizes the fact that such a separation has already occurred. Without seeing the natural-law basis of what Jesus is teaching, therefore, it is difficult to understand why he said what he said in this text.

Back to the Created Order: Churches and Pastors

Another explicit appeal to the created order to explain the Christian moral life appears in 1 Corinthians 9. Paul's broad goal in this text was to explain his own ministry among the Corinthian believers. One striking feature of his ministry is that he refused to receive financial remuneration from them: he presented "the gospel free of charge" (9:18). But Paul did not want them to think they should expect this from all ministers of the gospel. In fact, as a rule, "the Lord commanded that those who proclaim the gospel should get their living

---

[9] My interpretation of Matt 19:9 reflects that of the Westminster Confession of Faith, 24.5. For exegetical defense of this interpretation, see, for example, John Murray, *Divorce* (Phillipsburg, NJ: Presbyterian and Reformed, 1961), chap. 2. Some writers have argued, on the contrary, that this text doesn't justify remarriage after adultery. E.g., see William A. Heth and Gordon J. Wenham, *Jesus and Divorce: The Problem with the Evangelical Consensus* (Nashville: Thomas Nelson, 1984), 113–37.

by the gospel" (9:14). But Paul wanted to explain the rule rather than just state it. For this he looked primarily to the natural law.

He made his first and primary argument through three rhetorical questions: "Who serves as a soldier at his own expense? Who plants a vineyard without eating any of its fruit? Or who tends a flock without getting some of the milk?" (9:7). Paul relied on his readers' knowledge of how the world works. There is no point of asking these questions unless he could assume his readers knew that the answer to all three is obvious: almost no one acts in these ways. Governments that try to raise an army of entirely self-supporting soldiers will end up with a small and impoverished force. While an unusual individual may plant and tend a vineyard simply for the fun of it, most people will forgo the effort if they cannot eat its grapes, drink its wine, or at least be paid by those who do. It is similar for those tending a flock.

This is the natural order of things. People who work for others should be paid by them. People who work their own property have a right to its fruits. Such expectations are simply just. As Paul noted elsewhere in a different context, "to the one who works, his wages are not counted as a gift but as his due" (Rom 4:4). Such practices are even naturally necessary, we might say, at least most of the time. People who devote their energy to fighting wars or cultivating vineyards or tending flocks will not ordinarily be able to survive if they do not get compensated for these activities, because they do not have time or opportunity to make a living elsewhere. This is how the world works. These natural necessities pertain to ministers too, although their responsibilities go far beyond anything knowable through natural law. Pastors and their families need to eat, no less than soldiers and shepherds do. If churches want their ministers to devote themselves to pastoral work, in most cases they'll have to pay them for their efforts.

Paul confirms his reasoning through an analogy from the Mosaic law: "Does not the Law say the same? For it is written in the Law of Moses, 'You shall not muzzle an ox when it treads out the grain.' Is it for oxen that God is concerned? Does he not certainly speak for our sake?" (9:8–10). It would be interesting to reflect on how Paul used the Mosaic law here, but that would take us beyond our main concern. So, I simply note that Paul went to the natural law *first* and merely found *confirmation* of his natural-law conclusion from the Mosaic law. For all of the new and wonderful realities Christ's coming has brought to the people of God, they still live in the present world. The natural law cannot fully explain the Christian life (far from it!), but the Christian life is incomprehensible apart from it.

6

Learning the Natural Law and Engaging the Public Square

This book has considered a lot of evidence that the natural law exists and that sinful people, to various degrees, know what it teaches. But we have not spent much time on the question of how exactly people learn what the natural law communicates. This book has also reflected on how natural law serves as one of God's means for constraining sin in human societies. But we have not explored how Christians might engage the public square through appeals to the natural law. This final chapter addresses these two remaining issues.

My approach and conclusions may not be what readers expect. When many people hear the term "natural law," they associate it with sophisticated philosophical arguments. From this perspective, natural law is the domain of smart people who

develop irrefutable arguments that establish the correct view on
controversial moral issues. If this is what natural law is all about,
then learning the natural law requires rigorous academic training, and we should engage the public square by communicating sharp rational arguments. This perspective is understandable.
Philosophical discourse is in fact the context in which "natural
law" often appears.[1] And scholars sometimes present sophisticated natural-law arguments to the broader public to try to sway
public-policy debates.

But there are some serious difficulties with thinking about
natural law in this way. For one thing, it makes natural law in-
accessible to most individuals, who are not intellectuals. Few people
are interested in or capable of engaging in high-level philosophical arguments. When such arguments are presented to a general audience, they seem to have little effect on public opinion.[2]
Furthermore, associating natural law with philosophical argumen-
tation seems to be inconsistent with biblical claims that *all* people
know the content of natural law. It also seems inconsistent with
biblical stories describing ordinary people exhibiting the fear of
God or recognizing things that ought not to be done. I do not
claim that there is no place for intellectuals to develop sophisticated natural-law arguments. But there are real drawbacks to
thinking about natural law primarily in these terms. I wish to suggest a better way to think about learning the natural law and using
it to engage the public square.

---

[1] Among numerous examples, see Jonathan Crowe, *Natural Law and
the Nature of Law* (Cambridge: Cambridge University Press, 2019); and
Robert P. George, *In Defense of Natural Law* (Oxford: Clarendon, 1999).

[2] One example that comes to mind is Sherif Girgis, Ryan T. Anderson,
and Robert P. George, *What Is Marriage? Man and Woman: A Defense*
(New York: Encounter, 2012).

This chapter argues that people learn the natural law in much the same way that they mature in wisdom. We will turn back to Proverbs once again for insight. As previous chapters have noted, Proverbs largely instructs readers in wisdom by helping them gain deep understanding of how the world works and how to live effectively in such a world, given who we are as human beings. In other words, the acquisition of wisdom in Proverbs is much the same thing as gaining perception of the natural law. This means that what Proverbs tells us about how we mature in wisdom is also informative about how we learn the law of nature. We will see that learning the natural law is thus for ordinary people and not just for elites—for ordinary *thoughtful* people, to be sure, but not necessarily thoughtful in an academic way. We will also see that this learning process takes time, both for individuals and for communities. People gain knowledge of the natural law through long experience, and there are no intellectual shortcuts.

If ordinary people can and do learn the natural law, this implies that it is appropriate for Christians to appeal to it in the public square and that this has some possibility of success. At the same time, the fact that learning the natural law is a long process acquired through life experience should also temper our expectations. We need to guard against naïve optimism. Just because we can make a clever argument does not mean it will be persuasive to people who have been sidetracked in the process of learning the natural law. I will argue that these various considerations encourage us to use natural law flexibly in the public square, with realistic and moderate expectations.

To accomplish these objectives, the chapter will first discuss how we come to know the natural law, drawing on Proverbs especially. Then it offers some reflections and advice about engaging the public square accordingly.

Learning the Natural Law

Proverbs largely presents wisdom as perception of the natural moral order, that is, as deep understanding of how the world works and how to live well within it. Thus, seeing how Proverbs instructs us to gain wisdom also informs us how to learn the natural law.[3]

The fact that Proverbs presents wisdom as *perception* is worth initial reflection. Wisdom is a kind of knowledge, but not the only kind. Some knowledge is factual, for example. History teachers may want students to learn the dates of important events, and geography teachers may want students to learn the names and locations of great rivers. Students gain such factual knowledge through memorization. Teachers teach facts through presenting them, repeating them, and perhaps through suggesting memorization devices. But perception represents a different sort of knowing. How the world works is much too complicated and nuanced to be memorized. The world tends to work in certain ways, and human beings tend to respond in certain ways in certain circumstances, but there are exceptions. The world is characterized by patterns, not by ironclad causes and effects. To accomplish its goals effectively, the moral life must be attentive and responsive to these subtleties. In other words, wisdom entails a deep understanding—a perception—of tendencies, patterns, and exceptions. Thus, Proverbs teaches perception in a way distinct from the teacher presenting facts to memorize. Proverbs shows us how the world works and what wholesome and non-wholesome living within it looks like. It instills knowledge more than it imparts it. It helps us see what is going on in the sense

---

[3] For a more detailed discussion of the material in this section, and interaction with other writers, see PAC, 137–49.

of making readers say: "Oh . . . I see." This is how people learn the natural law.

One way Proverbs teaches in this way is by suggesting rules of conduct or of cause-and-effect but then also making clear that things do not always operate according to these rules. It does not tell us "Here are general rules" and "Here are the exceptions." Instead, it *shows* both to us. It places the rules and exceptions before us for our reflection. It tells us that those who work their land have plenty to eat while those who go after worthless pursuits have plenty of poverty (28:19). It says similar things repeatedly, implicitly urging readers toward an industrious life. We see a connection between righteous conduct and material prosperity. But Proverbs also alerts readers to the fact that some people become wealthy by crooked-ness and exploitation and that sometimes the righteous are poor (e.g., 28:6, 8). As we ponder such texts, which may strike us as contradictory at first, our minds put the pieces together. We begin to see the patterns and exceptions of the world and to get the feel of how to navigate them.

Proverbs also instills perception by depicting people's folly in concrete, graphic ways. As considered in the previous chapter, it is one thing to be told "don't commit adultery" and another to be shown how stupid and destructive it is. Thus, Proverbs not only gives general warnings against adultery but also paints the detailed scene of the young man seduced by the forbidden woman (7:6–23). Proverbs also does this with the economic issues I mentioned pre-viously. It helps us see industriousness and laziness for what they really are by comparing the sleeping sluggard to a door turning on its hinges (26:14), caricaturing the sluggard as too lazy to move his fork from plate to mouth (26:15), and describing the hardworking ant (6:6–11). People can memorize facts through rote learning techniques, but such concrete depictions help people take in and absorb the characteristics of a good life in this world.

Yet another way Proverbs teaches by showing is through analogizing human behavior to phenomenon in the natural world. Chapters 25–26 are filled with these types of examples. Among other things, these chapters liken various kinds of good and bad behavior to a bad tooth, vinegar on soda, the north wind, cold water, a polluted fountain, a city without walls, snow in summer, and a flitting sparrow. Such analogies appeal to what we already understand in nature to help us develop a taste for what kind of behavior is fitting or useful or destructive or tragic or bizarre or inappropriate and the like. We might say that it instills a *taste* for the true character of various sorts of conduct. The person who has memorized something can give a simple account of what he has learned: he can list the dates of a dozen historical events, for instance. But a person with taste cannot do this. A coffee connoisseur cannot really capture what makes a certain brew superior in a sentence or two, at least not to someone who does not also have superior taste, and a connoisseur of wine cannot communicate briefly to a general audience what distinguishes a good vintage from a great one. Proverbs seeks to entice us into developing a taste for superb moral living, into becoming a connoisseur of the natural law.

This perception of the natural order can only be gained over a long period of time. No one becomes a true connoisseur of coffee or wine by taking a crash course. Nothing can replace painstakingly thoughtful experience over years and decades. The same must be true for gaining a deep understanding of the natural law.

Proverbs confirms this intuition. It is apparently important that we begin learning the natural law from youth. The introductory section of Proverbs (chapters 1–9) reads as the instruction of a father to his son. It exhorts him repeatedly to get on the right moral path early in life, to lay aside the simple and foolish ways of youth, and to embrace the instruction and discipline of wisdom as his greatest asset. But Proverbs also makes clear that this learning process must continue into adulthood. People should keep seeking counsel, taking advice, and honoring their elders (e.g., 10:8; 12:15; 16:31; 20:29). The fact that Proverbs portrays older people as generally the wisest indicates that growing in wisdom does not end with early adulthood but continues into life's later stages. All of this also communicates the importance of humility for learning the natural law. Since we humans are always on the way, always having more to learn, always needing others' help, pride is sure to choke off the learning process. (This is also why the fear of God is such an important natural-law concept, as considered in chapter 3, since the fear of God and humility are so closely related. I return to this shortly.)

Furthermore, Proverbs teaches that this lifelong learning comes not only by listening to others wiser than oneself but also by a process of self-education. The experience required to learn the natural law involves *personal* experience. One should keep seeking counsel and taking advice, but it cannot stop there. We must also be in the trenches of life. We must try, fail, and learn from our mistakes. We should be alert, paying attention to what goes on around us and thereby developing a knack for how the world turns. Proverbs provides a snapshot of this process in 24:30–34: A person passes by the field of a sluggard, and this person is alert and attentive. "Behold," he says. He sees the sluggard's vineyard overgrown with thorns, its ground filled with weeds, and its stone wall crumbling. But he does not just notice this. He also reflects on it: "I saw and considered it; I looked and received instruction." Finally, he reaches a conclusion: Laziness is foolish. It leads to poverty. Observation, reflection, and conclusion—here is a crucial way to learn the natural law.

This perception of the natural law learned through experience over time resembles the kind of knowledge people have who are skilled in various activities. Examples include playing a musical instrument, speaking a foreign language, or playing a difficult sport. It does not take much time to memorize the rules of golf, proper etiquette on the course, or the names of different clubs. But someone who merely learns these basic facts does not really know golf. The person must play golf to gain such knowledge. She hits tens of thousands of shots, over thousands of rounds, on hundreds of courses, in dozens of different conditions to gain true expertise in golfing well. It helps to get advice from more experienced golfers who know what they are talking about. But it is also crucial to experience it for oneself through practice, observation, reflection, and conclusion. One must develop a reliable swing and a good touch for chipping and putting. Plus, there are countless variables affecting how one should play a given shot: how the ball lies on the ground, the direction and strength of the wind, whether the target is uphill or downhill, the temperature and humidity, whether more trouble lies in front, behind, or to one side of the target, and so on. The truly knowledgeable golfer may never face the same exact shot twice, but because she has hit shots in so many different circumstances, paid attention to the results, and reflected on other people's comments about their own experiences, she *just knows* how to approach a particular unique situation. The inexperienced golfer struggles to understand all the factors and to assess their relative importance, but the golfer with perception can evaluate the circumstances in a moment or two and know what shot and strategy is best. Occasionally, an especially difficult situation demands additional thought, but again the truly knowledgeable golfer can often figure out a way to hit a good shot, or at least avoid a bad one. Learning the natural law and putting it into practice is a lot like this.

Let's reflect on a couple of implications of what we have considered thus far. The first is that learning the natural law is a *communal* endeavor and not just an individual one. Yes, much depends on how well individuals heed instruction, are alert to the world, and reflect on experience. But note the communal element even in this. A person can hardly learn the natural law if he has no wise instruction to heed. As Proverbs indicates, the learning process ought to begin in childhood. One's prospects for success in this process are greatly enhanced by having good parents who teach and model wise adherence to the natural law—and one's prospects are greatly diminished by lacking such parents. Other communal elements are also a factor. Early on, Proverbs highlights how easily bad friends can derail a young person (1:10–19). Proverbs' instruction to seek counsel, take advice, and respect the elderly also presumes that there are wise people in one's social orbit. We might think as well of Paul's pithy maxim "Do not be deceived: 'Bad company ruins good morals'" (1 Cor 15:33; cf. Prov 13:20), which he probably borrowed from a pagan Greek writer as a piece of natural-law wisdom. Clearly, living in a wholesome moral environment does not guarantee that a person will learn the natural law well, nor does living in a destructive moral environment doom one to utter confusion about it, but it is difficult to overestimate the importance of people's social environment if they aspire to learn the natural law.

From this communal aspect of learning the natural law, the other implication follows, and it sets the stage for the second part of this chapter. It may be discouraging and sobering to say, but there is only so much that public appeals to natural law can do to counter a hostile moral environment. A good natural-law argument is not likely to persuade people who have been habituated from youth to follow and revel in destructive moral paths. To draw on analogies suggested above: One good tip will not turn a bad golfer into a scratch golfer overnight. A sip of good coffee or good wine may well repulse the person who has never tried coffee or wine. A person who does not already have a taste for the natural law probably will not appreciate even a brilliantly logical appeal to it.

This ought to give us modest expectations as we approach the subject of using natural law to engage the public square. In our own day, Christians face many cultural barriers to communicating the natural law effectively. Refining the intellectual rigor of our arguments has some value in certain settings but has few prospects for changing minds in daily interaction with unbelievers or in contemporary political diatribe. Yet although this section's conclusions point away from naïve optimism, they also reject nihilistic pessimism. We must remember that our contemporary societies have widely rejected many terrible practices, such as race-based slavery. Our economies produce amazingly beneficial items, and our legal systems deter and punish a great deal of injustice. Even people we regard as only mildly competent can cope in life to a remarkable degree. Amid much moral rot, our societies also embody an impressive degree of perception into how this world works and how to live productively in it. To return to our analogies: Most people are not coffee connoisseurs, but many drink average coffee and appreciate it. Most golfers cannot break par, but many of them figure out the basics and can work their way around a course without total embarrassment. What we have to work with in the public square is modest, but it is not nothing. Christians, who have many moral limitations of their own, ought to think about natural law and the public square accordingly.

Natural Law in the Public Square

It is important to clarify exactly what we are considering as we turn to the use of natural law in the public square. I wish to address how Christians might engage non-Christians on moral and political issues of common concern. But I am not addressing how Christians should *evangelize* non-Christians. Evangelization is one of the church's central purposes, as Jesus's Great Commission indicates (Matt 28:18–20). In what follows, I assume the importance of the Great Commission but discuss a different subject. God does not want Christians to dissociate themselves from non-Christians in earthly affairs (1 Cor 5:9–10). He calls us to live peacefully with them as far as possible (Rom 12:18). We live under the same political authorities as non-Christians (Rom 13:1) and work alongside and under them (1 Thess 4:11–12; 1 Pet 2:18).

This means that there is more to Christians' interaction with their unbelieving neighbors than just evangelizing them. Since we share neighborhoods, workplaces, governments, and much else with them, we have keen interest in how peacefully they live, how well they work, and how they evaluate what is just. As with the Israelite exiles in Babylon, so too for Christians as exiles in the world: when our surrounding society prospers, we will also, generally speaking (Jer 29:7; cf. 1 Pet 2:11). Thus, Christians rightly look for ways to promote what is good and just in their communities. Even if our unbelieving neighbors do not believe the gospel, we still want them to be industrious rather than lazy, sober rather than drunk, peaceful rather than violent, and married rather than cohabitating. The question before us then is how we can engage them in ways that promote such practices and habits, and specifically why and how to do so through the natural law.

A Perspective on the Use of Natural Law

I suggest first that Christians should be nondogmatic and flexible about the way they engage non-Christians in public affairs. The New Testament gives no specific instruction on how to engage them nor even any examples of early Christians doing so. It leaves this to our discretion. This makes things more challenging for us in a way, but it also frees us to be creative. It should also keep one Christian from being too quick to condemn fellow believers for making different judgments about how to pursue this engagement. Nevertheless, we do want to make sound and effective judgments, so it is worth giving this issue some thought.

Before considering the use of natural law, we might wonder about using *Scripture* in the public square. Nothing prohibits this, and there may be occasions when it is appropriate. But it is probably not the wisest or most effective strategy in most cases. Obviously, Christians proclaim Scripture when evangelizing, and Christians should surely discuss biblical teaching when speaking with each other about public affairs. But why would we appeal to Scripture when engaging unbelievers? One possibility is that Christians do so to feel good about themselves, as if it proves that they are not ashamed of Christ or afraid to be ridiculed. Few believers would likely want to admit to such motivations, but I suspect it often plays some role. It is not a good reason. Of course, Christians should never be ashamed of Christ, but the point of engaging unbelievers in the public square is not to bolster our spiritual self-esteem but to advance what is good and just in society. And there are strong reasons to think that appealing to Scripture usually will not further a Christian's public-policy goals. Appealing to Scripture (especially with the attitude of trying to prove one's unashamed loyalty to Christ) communicates that whatever moral point we are trying to prove is a *Christian* thing, since the Bible is Christians' holy book. Non-Christians do not regard Scripture as authoritative. If we say "the Bible teaches this moral position," non-Christians will logically conclude that this is what Christians believe but will also likely conclude that it is irrelevant for them. That is not what we should want to communicate when seeking to promote what is good and just in our societies. Such appeals to Scripture seem likely to drive a deeper moral wedge between believers and unbelievers, when what we seek is just the opposite. To put it another way: the goal of engaging non-Christians in the public square is to persuade them on moral and political issues of common concern, but appealing to Scripture is more likely to dissuade than to persuade.

Another reason why Christians might appeal to Scripture in this setting is simply because it is easier than other options. If one is dealing with public debates about sexuality, for example, it is easy to find biblical verses that teach the immorality of certain practices and lifestyles. We can recite these verses and be done with it without much effort. In contrast, trying to persuade non-Christians through appeals to the natural law is considerably more difficult and intimidating. How exactly does nature teach this or that? How can I communicate this point effectively? Answering these questions is neither obvious nor easy, but following this route is usually appropriate and possible.

It is appropriate because natural law is the moral standard Christians and non-Christians share. On the one hand, natural law addresses human beings *as human beings*. On the other hand, the New Testament says to readers: You have been raised with Christ; therefore, conduct yourselves in such and such a way (Col 3:1–5) and live lives worthy of your calling (Eph 4:1). That is, Scripture says: you are Christians, participants in God's salvation in Christ, so behave accordingly. In contrast, the natural law (in effect) says: you are human beings, creatures made in God's image, thus act in a fitting way. Natural law addresses non-Christians in a direct way that biblical commands generally do not.

Making natural-law appeals is possible (though challenging). If we really believe what Scripture teaches, then we believe that the testimony of natural law is powerful. It is clear enough to hold all people accountable on the day of judgment (Rom 1:20). We believe that at some level all people *know* the content of natural law and the just consequences of rejecting it (Rom 1:20–21, 32). Furthermore, there must be a considerable degree of natural-law perception embedded in our communities, at least for those of us who live in productive and functional societies that are mostly peaceful and protect against many kinds of injustice. Natural realities also constrain people from being as bad as they want to be. Many people tempted to commit adultery do not because they do not want the pain and loss of a family breakup. Many people tempted to be lazy keep working hard because they know they must eat: "A worker's appetite works for him; his mouth urges him on" (Prov 16:26).

In short, Christians face real challenges when engaging unbelievers with the natural law, but they also have a lot going for them. Christians have a stronger hand than they may think. They have reality on their side. Let's turn, then, to reflect on how we might utilize our advantages.

Strategies for Engaging through Natural Law

This final part of the book does not offer a comprehensive strategy for interaction in the public square. I do not claim to know any foolproof tactics. Here I simply suggest three considerations designed to stimulate readers' thinking and perhaps to inspire them to more winsome engagement with non-Christians on moral and political issues of common concern. (I do not think Christians need to announce in public that they are making "natural-law arguments." In fact, this may often be counterproductive. We can engage people on the basis of natural law without using the term.)

First, for effective natural-law engagement, Christians should surely wish to promote *humility* in the public square. As chapter 3 discussed, the presence or absence of the fear of God in a society is one of the prime factors in how well it protects and promotes what is just. Humility is the flip side of the fear of God. To the extent that people exalt themselves in pride, they raise their fists against the Almighty. As observed earlier in this chapter, the humble posture of learning from others, seeking counsel, and respecting the aged is crucial for acquiring wisdom from the natural order. There can be little doubt that the more humility a society exhibits, the more effective appeals to the natural law will be.

It is clear, however, that Christians often do not exude humility in the public square. Sinners are indisposed to humility, so it is no surprise that Christians often fail in this area. Yet there are some heightened temptations to pride and arrogance in public affairs today. Confronted with increasing moral relativism in our culture, Christians feel pressure to emphasize their nonrelativistic stance. Admitting that many issues are difficult or ambiguous can seem like compromise and cowardice. Moreover, the increasing polarization of politics is well recognized (certainly in my own American context, but in other places as well). On many issues, a considerable percentage of the population divides into two groups that take drastically different views and, at all costs and whatever the evidence, seek to vindicate their own group and discredit the other. Surrounded by so much noise and passion, it is easy for Christians to get sucked in.

To be sure, there are social controversies in which the moral issues are clear-cut. And political divisions may occasionally arise in which one side is wholly in the right and the other side wholly wrong. When so, Christians need to be resolute in standing for what is right. But even in these circumstances, they should do so humbly rather than arrogantly. Promoting the good cause in a way that communicates self-righteousness or self-promotion is hardly likely to persuade people who hold other views.

But I am more concerned to address situations when matters are complicated and nuanced rather than black-and-white. At times a moral issue is clear but how to deal with it politically is perplexing. Sometimes a likeable candidate takes a reprehensible policy position, and other times an unlikeable candidate takes a great policy position. Often, we strongly support a particular political cause but have to admit honestly that the other side has some valid concerns. Occasionally political divisions arise in which advocates of both sides make compelling arguments—and perhaps more often, both make lousy arguments. Under such circumstances, truth and goodness do not rest entirely with one candidate, one agenda, one party, or one movement. If we are really concerned about promoting justice, we should want all valid concerns to be recognized, we should want the ambiguities of bad-candidates-taking-good-positions (and vice versa) acknowledged rather than veiled, and we should want strong arguments on both sides to be heard and weak arguments on both sides exposed. Another way to put it is that societies are much more likely to find peaceful, just, and productive resolutions to difficult issues if as many participants as possible are humble enough to listen to others and reflect on their insights and shortcomings seriously.

Christians cannot miraculously produce such humility in their societies, obviously, but they can seek to promote it, or at least not hinder it. Christians can model this humility by being quick to listen and slow to speak, by acknowledging others' concerns even when we do not agree with their conclusions, and by refusing to absolutize the goodness or badness of people and agendas when no such absoluteness exists. In recent years, as I write this, public opinion regarding the presidency of Donald Trump and the COVID-19 pandemic have provided notorious examples of stark polarization, unnuanced rhetoric, and unrelenting attempts on both sides to discredit the opposition. Christians were not generally responsible for initiating such polarization, and many wise Christians have tried to avoid it and promote a humbler perspective that acknowledges concerns on both sides and rejects the distortions of both. But many Christians have been drawn into this divide and have exacerbated the rampant lack of humility. Surely few of us can say honestly that we could not have done better. To promote the cause of goodness and justice under the natural law, let us all strive to be humble and promote humility all the more.

Second, Christians might make effective natural-law arguments by taking advantage of the wholesome moral judgments their fellow citizens already make. There is not much to say to those who recognize nothing that is morally true, but most people are not like that. Why not begin with something they already acknowledge and try to show them that, if this one thing is true, other things must also be true?

A good example comes from controversies over abortion and protection of unborn human life. (What I am about to say concerns my own American context, but similar things may be true for non-American readers.) As contentious as abortion is in the United States, it is easy to overlook something for which Christians may give thanks: Americans overwhelmingly oppose infanticide, the killing of very young children *after* they are born. This is hardly something we can take for granted. Many societies in human history have practiced infanticide, including the Greco-Roman communities among which the new-covenant church first grew. There is a conviction in the United States that infanticide is *something which ought not to be done*, to borrow biblical words discussed in chapter 3. This is very good. But recognizing that a day-old baby is a human person with a right to life is simply inconsistent with recognizing a mother's right to abort a baby *in utero*.

We can see this, for example, by working backward in time.[4] There is nothing different about a baby an hour after it is born from what it was an hour before it was born. She simply lives out of the womb and eats and breathes on her own, which she was capable of doing a few hours earlier but had no opportunity to do. Nothing about that baby's nature has changed, physically or mentally, to justify a radical shift in her legal standing. But what about earlier in her fetal existence? We can keep moving the clock back and look for some point at which she changes from one sort of being into another. One might suggest the point of viability (which has been an important point of demarcation in much American abortion law). But in fact, there is no such point. We can never identify a line at which a fetus moves from being unviable to viable. Due to medical technology, we can now keep premature infants alive at a much earlier stage than in previous centuries, and future technology is likely to save them at even earlier stages. This alone is proof that there is no *inherent* point of viability in which a fetus changes from one sort of creature to another. But using viability as criterion has further difficulties. A fetus whose mother has access

---

[4] For a more detailed version of this argument, see David VanDrunen, *Bioethics and the Christian Life: A Guide to Making Difficult Decisions* (Wheaton, IL: Crossway, 2009), 158–65.

to excellent health care may be judged viable while another fetus of the same age and physical health might be judged nonviable because her mother lives in a poor, remote village. So it should be legal to kill the latter but not the former? (Another disadvantage for poor people!)

We could keep going back in time and hunt for another decisive point in which the fetus becomes something she was not before. What we would find is a lot of remarkable development over a relatively short period of time, but nothing like a radical shift into some other kind of being. That is, there is no such shift until we reach one point where we clearly do find it: fertilization. Before fertilization, there are two entities, a sperm and an egg, each of which obviously is not a human being and has zero potential to grow into one. But once they combine, a new being comes into existence, with a unique genetic makeup and the ability to move through the process of human development.

Will every non-Christian who rejects infanticide, who hears such an argument in the public square, acknowledge that human life begins and should be protected from conception? Of course not. Is it an argument that has promise to prick the conscience of some relatively humble non-Christians who hear it and to convince them to change their view on abortion for the better? Yes, it is. It has much better promise than quoting a biblical text to them.

Finally, I suggest that Christians can make effective natural-law appeals by using empirical evidence—carefully. Making careless gestures to empirical evidence might make Christians look stupid and may open them to charges of violating the is-ought fallacy discussed in chapter 2. But I do suggest that empirical evidence can contribute to natural-law engagement in the public square.

It is not that empirical evidence *proves* what the natural law is in any strict or direct way. But if the natural law exists, and thus if the world is meaningful, purposeful, and orderly, then we would expect things to go better in life for those who obey the natural law, all else being equal. If working hard runs with the grain of the universe, for example, it should bring more prosperity than laziness does. If this is so, we should take advantage of it when engaging unbelievers. Pointing to the naturally good results that follow from naturally good conduct need not be done mechanistically (as if whatever increases a country's economic growth is necessarily morally good). But as a way at least to alert people to the harm their evil conduct does, it has a valid place in engaging the public square.

I mention just one example, and this, too, seeks to capitalize on good things most people already acknowledge. Changing sexual and familial norms is another highly controversial issue of recent years. Yet one thing has remained constant: most people love their children. At least, they want their children to succeed in life rather than fail. They want them to finish school, not get pregnant as a teenager, stay off drugs, and get a good job. Again, we can hardly take this for granted. Some parents abuse or abandon their children. But we can be grateful that this is not true for most.

In recent decades, all sorts of sociological studies have been released showing that, on every widely accepted measure of life success, children growing up in homes in which their biological mother and father are married to each other do far better than in any other family arrangement.[5] Most of these studies were done by non-Christians, and many of them by people who are not morally opposed to non-traditional family structures. But the evidence can

---

[5] E.g., see discussions in Robert D. Putnam, *Our Kids: The American Dream in Crisis* (New York: Simon & Schuster, 2015); and Charles Murray, *Coming Apart: The State of White America 1960–2010* (New York: Crown Forum, 2012). Cf. PAC, 225–27.

hardly be denied. Will such evidence convince society to overturn the sexual revolution altogether? Highly doubtful. Those who have been raised on a diet of sexual permissiveness and the glamor of choosing one's own way of life will be hard to convince. And since some children who grow up in nontraditional homes stay sober and get good jobs, anyone can convince himself that *his* children will do fine in a non-traditional arrangement. But can appeals to such evidence make an impression on some people who genuinely care about their own kids as well as the physical, mental, and financial health of the next generation? Yes, surely it can.

Conclusion

As we come to the end of this brief study, I hope readers will have gained new appreciation for the importance of natural law for Christians. Acknowledging the natural law is one way we confess that God has created and now sustains a world full of meaning, purpose, and order. Natural law is one of God's chief means for maintaining a measure of peace and justice in this fallen world. It explains how God is just in bringing all the world before his righteous judgment and ensures that the gospel of Christ is relevant and understandable to everyone who hears it. Understanding the natural law also remains crucial for Christians seeking to live righteously in this world. And finally, as just considered, natural law provides a way for Christians to engage non-Christians in the public square with theological integrity and with some modest hope of success. Neither natural law itself nor our appeals to it will ever bring utopia. That has never been God's purpose in revealing natural law. But may we Christians be grateful for its abiding testimony to God's righteousness and the various blessings it brings as he governs this world toward its appointed end.

READING
RECOMMENDATIONS

The following list is designed to provide a range of examples of theological approaches to natural law from different traditions. The perspective of each book is noted in parentheses. I do not endorse everything in all these books.

Robert C. Baker and Roland Cap Ehlke, eds., *Natural Law: A Lutheran Reappraisal* (St. Louis: Concordia, 2011) (Lutheran).

J. Daryl Charles, *Retrieving the Natural Law: A Return to Moral First Things* (Grand Rapids: Eerdmans, 2008) (evangelical).

Jonathan Crowe and Constance Youngwon Lee, eds., *Research Handbook on Natural Law* (Northampton, MA: Edward Elgar, 2019) (general reference work).

Stephen J. Grabill, *Rediscovering the Natural Law in Reformed Theological Ethics*, Emory University Studies in Law and Religion (Grand Rapids: Eerdmans, 2006) (Reformed).

Russell Hittinger, *The First Grace: Rediscovering the Natural Law in a Post-Christian World* (Wilmington, DE: ISI, 2003) (Roman Catholic).

Matthew Levering, *Biblical Natural Law: A Theocentric and Teleological Approach* (Oxford: Oxford University Press, 2008) (Roman Catholic).

David Novak, *Natural Law in Judaism* (Cambridge: Cambridge University Press, 1998) (Jewish).

David VanDrunen, *Natural Law and the Two Kingdoms: A Study in the Development of Reformed Social Thought* (Grand Rapids: Eerdmans, 2010) (Reformed).

————, *Divine Covenants and Moral Order: A Biblical Theology of Natural Law* (Grand Rapids: Eerdmans, 2014) (Reformed).

————, *Politics after Christendom: Political Theology in a Fractured World* (Grand Rapids: Zondervan Academic, 2020) (Reformed).

SUBJECT INDEX

A

Aaron, 49
Abimelech, 39–47, 58, 74
abortion, 115–17
Abraham, 38–48, 58, 66
accountability, 8, 42, 74
adultery, 41, 54, 85–87, 91, 96, 103, 112
alcohol, 88–89
Amalekites, 51, 64
Ammon, 64, 66
Ammonites, 66
Amos, 34–36, 65–67
anger, 32, 64, 66, 89–90
Artaxerxes (king), 50

B

Babylon, 16, 50, 63–64, 81, 109
Barton, John, 34
behavior, 32, 44, 46, 56, 64, 70, 85–86, 88, 104

C

Cain, 27

Calvin, John, 12, 95
case law, 53, 82–83
children, 3, 37, 50, 115, 118–19
Christ, xii, 2–3, 5–6, 14, 29, 40, 57, 59–60, 69, 71, 74–77, 80–81, 86, 90–91, 93, 98, 110–12, 119
Christian life, natural law and, 80–98
churches, xi–xiii, 2, 13–14, 38, 56–57, 61, 75, 81, 84, 92–93, 96–98, 109, 116
civil authority, constraining of, 47–48
civil communities, Christians within, 3
civil government, 55
civil law, 3, 12, 14, 54, 82, 84, 95
Code of Hammurabi, 54
compassion, 84
conduct, rules of, 103
confidence, loss of, 19
cosmic nonsense, 34–36

Mosaic law, 12, 39, 49, 52–55,
  60, 67, 73–76, 82–83,
  92–95, 98
Moses, 12, 48–49, 53, 73, 76,
  82, 94–95, 98

N

natural law
  defined, 1–2, 6
  importance of, 11, 15–16,
    34, 45, 52, 79, 119
  learning as communal
    endeavor, 107
  learning of, 101–9
  limitations of, 80
  as moral standard, 111–12
  within philosophical dis-
    course, 100
  within public square, 108–19
  within Scripture, 4–5
  strategies for engaging,
    112–19
  testimony of, 13, 15, 37, 39,
    44, 51, 59–60, 112
  theory of, 6–9
  use perspective regarding,
    110–12
natural revelation, 6–9, 16, 38,
  51, 55, 60, 69–70, 83, 92
Near Eastern law, 52–55
Nebuchadnezzar (king), 50
new-covenant church, 38, 92,
  116
new creation, 5, 77
New Testament
  conservative nature of ethics
    within, 90–92

  natural law within, 55–57,
    90–98
Nineveh, 64
Noah, 27–30
Noahic covenant, 26–30, 37, 41,
  59, 62

O

omnipotence of God, 1–2
omniscience of God, 1
oracles
  of judgment, 61–62
  prophetic, against Gentile
    nations, 61–68

P

pagan society, natural law and,
  52
parenting, 118–19
pastors, 81, 96–98
Paul (apostle), 7–8, 11, 52,
  55–57, 60, 68–77, 81, 93,
  95–98, 107
perception, 83, 101–5, 106, 108,
  112
personal experience, learning
  natural law through, 105
Pharaoh, 48, 50
Pharisees, 93–96
politics, divisions within, 113–14
postmodernism, 18, 25
premodern culture, 18
prophetic oracles, against Gentile
  nations, 61–68
prosperity, 103, 118
Proverbs, 16, 22, 30–34, 80–90,
  101–5, 107

public square, natural law within
the, 92, 100–101, 108–19

Q

quarrels, 89–90

R

Rachel, 46
rage, 85, 90
rape, 45–47
reason, human, 8–10, 18
Reformation, 10–15, 17, 79
resurrection, 2, 77, 91
Roman council, 55–56
Rome, 10–16

S

salvation, 2, 30, 61, 69, 74, 76,
93, 112
Sarah (wife of Abraham), 40–41,
43, 45
Scotus, Duns, 13–14
Scripture
natural law within, 4–5
in the public square, 110–11
revelation of, 6–7
Shechem, 45–47
sin, 5, 7, 13, 15, 20, 26, 30,
35–37, 43, 52, 57, 60, 62,
64–65, 69–70, 73–75, 79,
85–87, 89–91, 95, 99. *See
also specific types*
sluggard, 32, 88, 103, 105
Sodom, 39, 42, 63

sojourning, 40–41, 45, 58
special revelation, 6, 16, 38, 44,
51, 60

T

Ten Commandments, 12
Thomas Aquinas, 8, 13–14
tolerance, 18
Trump, Donald, 115
Turretin, Francis, 13
Tyre, 63–66

U

unborn babies, 115–17
Ur, 43

W

wealth, 103
William of Ockham, 13–14
wisdom, 16, 22, 30–34, 53, 56,
81, 85, 95, 101–2, 105, 107,
113
world
creation of, 20–25
loss of confidence within, 19
meaning and purpose within,
17–20
natural order of, 33, 97–98
patterns within, 102

Z

Zedekiah (king), 50
Zephaniah, 63–64

SCRIPTURE INDEX